WATERFALL WALKS
AND DRIVES
in the
WESTERN CAROLINAS

D1598762

Published by
H. F. Publishing
4552 E. Elmhurst Dr.
Suite A
Douglasville, Ga. 30135
U.S.A.

I.S.B.N. 0-9636070-1-4

I dedicate this book to Robert J. Ringer, whose books have taught me what freedom really is, and to the founding fathers of this country, and to those who hold their principles dear.

Many thanks to James Bowen, Kevin O' Brien, Dee M. M. and the many rangers and strangers for their help with this book.

Line art by my railroading buddy Ron Noles.

Color Plates: Front cover, Linville Falls; back, Lower Falls, Slickrock Creek (Joyce Kilmer-Slickrock Wilderness).

<u>INTRODUCTION</u>

When people from this region think of waterfalls, usually Looking Glass or Whitewater Falls come to mind. These locations are very popular because of their beauty and easy access. My intentions, however, are to lead the reader to the lesser-known waterfalls in addition to the more popular locations. I appreciate the "lesser knowns" for the solitude they provide. Many of them have beauty that rivals or even exceeds that of the popular spots. Most of them are easily reached, requiring only a little more driving or footwork. By using a little common sense, they can be safely seen.

I enjoy researching the lesser knowns, then ferreting them out. Taking a topo map and finding my way through strange woods is a real challenge to the skills I acquired as a land surveyor. Surveying is a profession that I've been out of for many years, but it's still in my blood. I love landscape photography and hiking as well, so everything just fell in place, with the end result being this book.

Waterfalls are the "Gemstones of the East." Each one is faceted in different ways. Some have beauty that is big and bold, others have delicate and subtle characteristics. Common natural occurrences: rock, wood, and water reach their highest form when they come together as a waterfall. People who can't agree on anything else, seem to always agree on the beauty of a waterfall.

Although I know that I'm not the first to see them, there are some locations that are so pristine that I feel like I just may be the first. I have visited at least 200 waterfalls. In doing so, I've obtained directions from handouts, old timers, and rangers. All too often the handouts ended up just getting me lost. I have experienced the frustration of being several miles down a road, only to find that I could go no further because of unknown road conditions, etc., while still facing miles of driving to a trailhead. I also dislike being deep into a hike only to find I can go no further, account of high water or some other unknown obstacle. If I had only known the possible conditions beforehand, I might have altered my plans (waiting a few days for waters to recede after a rain for instance). I wrote these books to provide accurate information, so that you can make the most of your time. I wish you hours of hiking enjoyment. May your feet stay forever dry.

LIKE ANY OUTDOOR ACTIVITY, "WATERFALL WALKING" ISN'T WITHOUT ITS HAZARDS. THERE HAVE BEEN SEVERAL DEATHS AND INJURIES OF THOSE TRYING TO GET A CLOSER LOOK. NEVER JEOPARDIZE YOUR SAFETY BY GETTING INTO SOMETHING YOU CAN'T GET OUT OF. SAFETY MUST BE FIRST AND FOREMOST.

Rock climbing, spelunking, whitewater rafting and the like, have their own rules to minimize the risk of injury. "Waterfall Walking" has its common sense rules too.

PLEASE REMEMBER THESE DON'TS:
1. DON'T VENTURE NEAR THE CLIFF EDGE FROM WHICH THEY FALL. THERE IS NO SCENERY OVER THE EDGE, SO WHY TAKE A CHANCE?
2. DON'T GET IN THE WATER ABOVE THEM.
3. DON'T BE FOOLED BY THE APPEARANCE OF SOLID GROUND. MOST OF THESE WATERFALL AREAS STAY PERPETUALLY WET FROM MIST, AND HAVE A THIN LAYER OF LEAVES OR TOP-SOIL HIDING *ALWAYS* SLICK ROCK.
4. DON'T CLIMB THEM.
5. DON'T LEAVE VALUABLES IN YOUR CAR.
6. DON'T BLOCK GATES.

But please remember to:
1. Take your camera along.
2. Bring along books on wildflowers, birds, and trees because I assure you that you'll be scratching your head, pondering the strange and beautiful sights, seen as you trek through the woods en route to these waterfalls.
3. Haul out the litter that the inconsiderate have hauled in, leaving these sites naturally unaltered.

DISCLAIMER

The author and the publisher disclaim any liability or loss incurred as a consequence, directly or indirectly, of the use and application of any information contained in this book.

* * * * *

All distances in this book have been measured with a Rolatape measuring wheel.

All of the waterfalls contained in this book except Issaqueena Falls, S.C., are located on, and accessible via public lands. Issaqueena Falls is privately held, I have obtained permission to publish its location.

I have hiked to, but intentionally left out, Catawba, Connestee, and Harper Falls because of intervening private lands.

HIKING ESSENTIALS

- Drinking water
- Waterproof matches
- Good light hiking boots
- Flashlight
- High-energy foods
- Pocket knife
- Compass
- First-aid kit, with Benadryl or similar medicines for reactions to stings. Moleskin for blisters.
- Snake bite kit and knowledge on its use.

CONTENTS

HOW TO USE THIS BOOK

This text is keyed to its maps and begins near Murphy, North Carolina, then progresses eastward. After covering western North Carolina, the book takes in the stunning western portion of South Carolina.

This book will lead you from a prominent landmark or intersection to individual waterfalls. Where there are several waterfalls in close proximity to each other, they are listed in the order in which they are encountered from that landmark or intersection (see Holly Springs—Longcreek Area pg. 92).

Note in this example that #2 Brasstown Road is 11.9 miles from the intersection of U.S. Hwys. 76 West and 123 South in Westminster, S.C., via Hwy. 76, and that #5, the Chattooga River Bridge (Ga./S.C. state line) is 17.9 miles. To find the distance between them, simply subtract. The two points are 6 miles apart. In the same example if you wanted to drive from #5, the Chattooga River Bridge, to #3, Damascus Church Road, your distance would be 17.9 minus 13.2 equaling 4.7 miles.

Listed along with each waterfall is:

(1) The worst road conditions encountered: Graveled, etc. (See the example below.)

(2) A beauty scale of 1 (worth seeing), through 10 (a knockout).

(3) The waterfall's height (if known).

(4) The U.S.G.S. topographic map on which the waterfall is shown.

(5) The official trail number (if known).

(6) The one-way hiking distance, and/or time required to reach them (unless noted in the text).

(7) Water crossings (if any) and the effort needed to reach the falls (easy, through difficult). See definitions.

---

(1) Roads: Graveled   (2) A "10"   (3) 30'
(4) U.S.G.S. Quadrangle: Holly Springs, S.C.
(5) Trail #, (6) .8 of a mile, (7) water crossing, moderate

DEFINITIONS:

Easy: A hike with no appreciable grades.

Moderate: A hike with gentle grades.

Difficult: A hike with steep grades.

Graveled: A road that most automobiles without airdams could negotiate, except where noted.

High Clearance: A road that most pickup trucks could negotiate.

U.S.G.S. Quadrangle: A U.S. Geological Survey topo map.

ABBREVIATIONS:

BT= The Bartram Trail.

FT= The Foothills Trail.

CRT= The Chattooga River Trail.

F.S.= Forest Service, designating a Forest Service road.

S.R.= State Route. In the Carolinas many state routes are identified with numbers along with the road's name. For example Damascus Church Road in Longcreek, S.C., is also S.R. 37-96. In North Carolina, state route identification numbers are usually placed on the wooden post of a sign, such as a stop sign.

KEY TO MAP SYMBOLS:

★ = A landmark from which the text begins or ends.

A,1,b, etc.: Italicized letters or numbers on area maps represent waterfall locations or landmarks with mileages given in the text. Numbers subdivide capital letters; lower case letters subdivide numbers, etc.

Contour intervals on hiking maps are 200' unless otherwise noted.

▬▬▬▬▬▬	Paved Roads
▬ ▬ ▬ ▬ ▬	Graveled or Dirt Roads
▬ ▬ ▬ ▬	Trails
▬ • • • ▬	Rivers and Creeks
P	Parking

PHOTOGRAPHING WATERFALLS

Start with a good 35 mm SLR camera system. I prefer a manual camera such as the Nikon FM-2 for its simplicity and wide array of available accessories. Nikon also makes a 24-50 mm wide-angle zoom lens which is ideal for waterfall photography. Many of these waterfalls have to be photographed closely because of view-blocking rocks, trees, and vegetation. The 46 degree field of view of a normal lens (50 mm) in most cases is not wide enough.

Use a tripod and shutter-release cable at all shutter speeds. This eliminates the possibility of camera shake and ensures the sharpest images. This also allows you to make long exposures for smooth-flowing, velvet-like water.

Stop the lens down. Apertures of f 8 to f 22 give the greatest sharpness. Learn how to set the depth of field (hyperfocal distance) for any given aperture. It's very simple to do and you can obtain images that are sharp from front to back by setting your lens properly. For example on my 28 mm lens set at f 11, if I set the far depth of field distance (infinity in this example) in line with f 11 on the far depth of field scale, the near depth of field distance automatically lines up with f 11 on the *near* depth of field scale, and reads 5 feet. This means that all objects between 5 feet and infinity will be in sharp focus. Even though the scene appears out of focus in the viewfinder, it will be rendered on film with front-to-back sharpness. Compose the shot with this in mind, keeping objects that are too close (since they would be rendered out of focus on film) out of the frame. Better cameras like the FM-2 have a depth of field preview button to let you see the stopped-down results in advance.

Metering: Try to shoot in evenly lighted conditions. High contrast lighting produces poor photos. Master photographer Galen Rowell teaches that "...our eyes have an eleven-stop light range..." and that films simply can't record this wide tonal range. In order to come away with the best images we need to "...learn to see as the film sees...."

Print films can "see" a range of light, or have a *latitude* of 7 stops, with 5 stops being optimum. Slide films have a 5 stop latitude, with 3 being optimum. Meter your subject with this in mind. If there is an area in the viewfinder that is either too bright, or too dark, recompose the shot to eliminate the unwanted area. Remember that with most cameras the viewfinder only covers around 93 percent of a scene.

When metering, leave the waterfall out of the equation. Meter for the "averagely" lit rock and/or foliage around the waterfall. If you meter for the much brighter waterfall itself, you'll end up with gray water and silhouettes of the surroundings.

When using slow films in very low-light conditions, you can obtain a useable shutter speed by switching the camera's film speed dial to a faster film speed setting. If for instance you are using 50 speed film, set the aperture on your lens to obtain the depth of field you desire, then set the film speed dial to, let's say, 200 (used here for ease of calculation, you can use 100, 400, 1000, or whatever film speed setting it takes to get a reading). Take a meter reading of an averagely lit area in the scene. Now multiply that reading by 4, since 50 divided into 200 = 4. If you had a shutter speed reading of say, 1 second, expose the film for 4 seconds. If your camera's shutter speed dial doesn't allow for exposures of over 1 second, set the dial to the "bulb" setting and time the shot yourself, by counting, one thousand one, one thousand two, etc. Be sure to reset the film speed dial back to your correct film speed setting.

Call or write the film's manufacturer for a film data sheet which gives details of reciprocity failure. Reciprocity failure is the failure of film to record true colors when exposed for longer (or shorter) periods than it was designed for. With Fujichrome 50 and 100 speed films there is no correction needed for exposures of 4 seconds or less. With Kodachrome 25 and 64 speed films add 1/2 and 1 stop respectively when exposing at 1 second.

Exposure: To show the power of a large waterfall, stop the action with the use of a medium speed film ISO 100 or 200 and a fast shutter speed, 1/125th of a second or faster. Plan to shoot on a bright sunny day so that the sharper, small apertures can be used. Large, powerful waterfalls in general (but not always), look unnatural when long exposures are used.

Smaller waterfalls photograph better under shady or overcast conditions. This allows the use of small apertures for sharpness and long exposures to softly blur the water. Use films rated ISO 25 to 100 for their long exposure tolerances and fine grain. It's hard to obtain good shots on windy days using slow shutter speeds unless you can exclude the movement of vegetation.

Bracket your shots. Expose at the correct meter reading, then expose 1 stop over and 1 stop under in 1/2 stop increments. This assures that you'll have at least one correctly exposed shot.

Composition: Fill the frame with your subject. I have often made the mistake of trying to include too much in a photo, with the end result being a dinky waterfall lost among the other detail.

The "rule of thirds" works well in waterfall photography. This common composition technique catches, then leads the eye into a photo. Divide the viewfinder into thirds with two imaginary vertical lines and then two imaginary horizontal lines—like a tic-tac-toe board. When shooting either vertically or horizontally place the subject at or near one of the 4 positions where these lines cross. Compose the shot with the waterfall flowing freely into and across the frame.

Avoid "Keystoning" if possible. This occurs when the camera is tilted up or down. (But in the case of most waterfalls we will be at the base looking upward.) Since the subject is closer to the film plane at the bottom and farther away at the top, it appears much bigger at the bottom and smaller at the top (like a pyramid, or inverted keystone) than our eyes see it. Wide-angle lenses exaggerate this distortion. To avert this, try shooting the subject straight on (parallel) if possible. There are perspective-control lenses to correct this distortion, but they are expensive.

Films: I almost always shoot slide film for the sharpness and intense colors it is capable of recording. I'm partial to Fujichrome 50 and 100 speed films for their fine grain, true colors, and ease of processing.

The very best print films are Kodak Ektar 25 and 100 speed. Ektar films have fine grain, great sharpness, and excellent colors.

To learn more, I suggest you read "Galen Rowell's Vision." This is without a doubt the best book that I've read on landscape photography. Mr. Rowell's 35 mm photos, aside from being beautiful, have the sharp, crisp clarity of a larger film format.

Nantahala National Forest

The Nantahala National Forest is North Carolina's largest with over one-half million acres. Cherokee for land of the noonday sun, the name "Nantahala" was given to the river and its gorge which only taste light when the sun is high overhead.

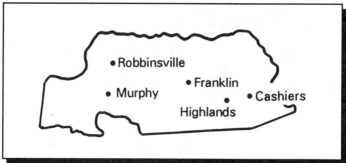

In this region you'll find waterfalls that require only the effort of driving, such as Cullasaja and Bridal Veil, or their hard to reach counterparts, Sassafras and Lower Falls on Slickrock Creek.

This area is home to the graceful and the mighty. Whitewater Falls at 411' is thought to be the highest in the eastern U.S. During the winter when the creeks and rivers are running at their highest levels, one can hear the constant roar of Whitewater Falls almost one-half mile away.

I especially enjoyed the Nantahala's Snowbird Area. In the fall, the drive along F.S. 75 is blazing in the orange of spotted touch-me-nots. Along one of the streamside trails you might pass the somewhat rare cardinal flower, whose chief pollinator is the hummingbird. You'll probably hear, but rarely see the pileated woodpecker whose jungle-like cuk-cuk-cuk-cuk-cuk call announces its presence.

At both Sassafras and Big Falls you'll notice potholed rock. These holes are caused by stones being trapped in one spot by larger stones, then being jackhammered in place by the water's actions.

1

Murphy Area

Leatherwood Falls Loop Trail, Clay County, N. Carolina

Roads: Graveled   A"1"
U.S.G.S. Quadrangle: Hayesville, N.C.
Trail #73, .8 of a mile, moderate

Directions: Where U.S. Hwy. 64 splits from U.S. Hwys. 19/129/74 just east of Murphy, drive east on U.S. 64 for 9.6 miles to S.R. 1302 (sign: Fires Creek Recreation Area). Turn left (north) and cross the Hiwassee River Bridge. Drive a total of 3.9 miles to a graveled road

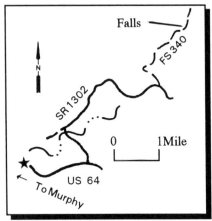

shown on the map of the Nantahala National Forest as F.S. 340, which is on the left (sign: Fires Creek 2 miles). In 1.9 miles, cross Fires Creek on a bridge and immediately turn left into the parking area.

The loop trail doesn't offer a full view of the falls. However, they may be partially seen from the parking area by looking across Fires Creek and northwest up the Leatherwood Branch Cove. To see them fully, you'll have to wade the bone chilling creek. When I visited this area, the creek was down, having only one deep spot. Winter and spring rains would make a crossing of Fires Creek dangerous.

The trail begins at the information board near the north end of the parking area.

Hike the trail upstream and in 200' cross Fires Creek on an iron footbridge. The Leatherwood Loop and the Cover Trail share the same paved treadway here. Sixty-five feet from the bridge the trails split. Turn left (west) on the Leatherwood Loop. The Cover Trail continues straight ahead.

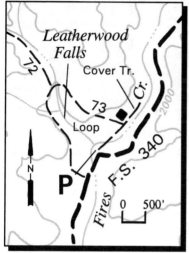

At .1 of a mile, in the vicinity of the outhouse, the pavement ends. The Leatherwood Loop turns sharply left here and begins ascending the mountainside. In another 700' arrive at the fall's observation deck. About all to be seen here are cascades.

Three-tenths of a mile into the hike, cross Leatherwood Branch on a footbridge. Soon you'll intersect the Fires Creek Rim Trail (#72). The Leatherwood Loop now turns downstream. In .3 of a mile, arrive back at F.S. 340 near the bridge crossing Fires Creek. Turn left and continue 400' back to the parking area.

Topton Area

Falls in the Nantahala Gorge, Macon County, N. Carolina

Roads: Paved   A "4" & A "4" respectively
U.S.G.S. Quadrangles: Topton/Hewett, N.C.
Seen from car

Directions: From the intersection of U.S. Hwys. 19/74 and 129 in the community of Topton, drive north on U.S. 19/74 for 2.1 miles to the community of Beechertown. Turn right (east) onto

S.R. 1412/1310 (sign: Nantahala River Launch Site) and drive up the Nantahala River Gorge. In approximately 3.7 miles, arrive at

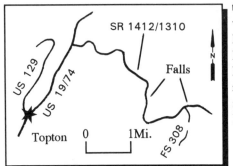

the first of two pullouts with beautiful over-looks of the cascading Nantahala River. Drive a total of 4.3 miles to a pullout on the right for Whiteoak Falls.

Whiteoak Falls

Seen from the shoulder of the road, this waterfall cascades over a jagged rock face. Mustard-colored lichens adorn a rock wall on the far side of the creek. Notice how the creek bed has been worn smooth by the water's abrasiveness.

A distant frontal view can be had from F.S. 308. To reach this viewpoint, drive .1 of a mile downstream, turn left, cross the bridge spanning Whiteoak Creek and park on its south side. A slim path leads up the north side of the creek to the base area.

Falls on Camp Branch

Seen from a pullout on the right (east) side of the Nantahala Gorge, 1.5 miles *downstream* from Whiteoak Falls.

Winter offers the best views here. The lower tier can be seen year-round. The upper tier is hidden from view by vegetation in the warm months. When the sun hits just right it's a total whiteout.

Snowbird—Tapoco Area

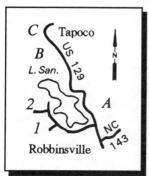

Directions: From the intersection of U.S. Hwy. 129 and N.C. Hwy. 143 in Robbinsville, N. Carolina, drive north on 129 to the following points of interest:

A. Massey Branch Road (S.R. 1116): 1.45 miles. Take S.R. 1116 for 3.5 miles to access (1) the falls in the Snowbird Area (see map below) and (2) the falls in the Joyce Kilmer—Citico Creek Area. (See map pg. 11.)

B. Big Fat Gap Road (F.S. 62), access to Wildcat Falls via the Big Fat Trail: 14.15 miles. (See map "B-C" pg. 14.)

C. Parking and trailhead for the Slickrock Creek Trail, access to Lower Falls: 15.9 miles. (See map "B-C" pg. 14.)

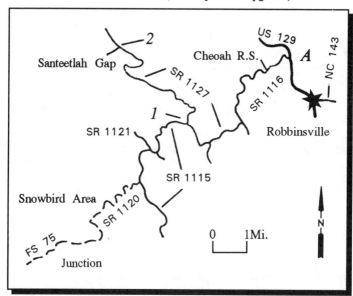

1. Snowbird Area,
Graham County, N. Carolina

Roads: Graveled
U.S.G.S. Quadrangle: Santeetlah Creek, N.C.
Trails: 64, 64A, & 65, 3.6 miles minimum, water crossings, moderate

---

This area was one of North Carolina's last to be settled by white men. In the 1830's settlements were established in the area north of Mouse Knob. In 1838 many Cherokee took refuge in the area's remoteness, while others were banished to Oklahoma on the infamous "Trail of Tears." Some of their descendants still reside in the area. In 1908 a 1600 acre game reserve was established by a Mr. George Moore. Wealthy hunters paid to bag exotic animals brought in from both the western states and from abroad. The venture failed when many of the animals were poached or escaped. In the 1920's the Bemis Hardwood Lumber Company bought lands in the region for its virgin timbers. By 1942 over 100 million board feet of lumber had been hauled out by rail. The Snowbird Area was purchased by the Forest Service in 1943 and the land has made an astonishing comeback.

Today, some of the area's trails follow the railroad beds which fed the Buffalo-Snowbird Railroad. Many trails still have the crossties in place. Trestles spanned many of the creeks, hollows, and ravines. En route to Sassafras Falls the trail makes several dips where the hollows were spanned by these trestles.

There are four waterfalls on the Snowbird Area trail map. Visiting all four in a day's time should be attempted by only the most seasoned hiker. The minimum hiking distance (to either Sassafras or Big Falls) is 3.6 miles one-way.

Directions: The Snowbird Area is reached from the intersection of Massey Branch Road (S.R. 1116/N.C. 143) and Snowbird Road (S.R. 1127/N.C. 143) by driving north on S.R. 1127/N.C. 143 for 2.1 miles. Turn left (west) onto S.R. 1115 (also called Snowbird Road) and in 2.1 miles arrive at a three-way intersection. (At this location S.R. 1115 bends sharply left, retaining its route number, after being intersected from the right by S.R. 1121.) Turn sharply left and continue 1 additional mile. After crossing Snowbird Creek on a concrete bridge, turn right onto S.R. 1120 which upon entering the Nantahala National Forest changes to F.S. 75. Drive 6.15 miles to its end, at Junction, which at one time was the railhead for the

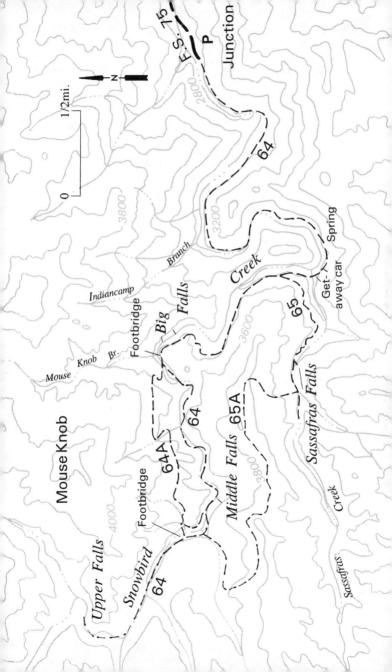

Buffalo-Snowbird Railroad. The trail, if not marked, is 50' to the left of the information board (the southernmost trail).

Big Snowbird Trail (#64): As you enter the woods this blue-blazed trail passes over numerous jeep blocking mounds. Soon it becomes more conducive to hiking—gently ascending alongside Snowbird Creek. In .7 and again at .8 of a mile cross small creeks. At 1.5 miles pass a jeep blocking boulder. Soon, the trail ascends slightly, then at mile 2.3 levels out as you approach a piped spring. Two and one-half miles into the hike, arrive at an open area with a confusing "Y" intersection. Disregard the path on the left. Take the trail to the right (north) and in 30' notice the "get-away car" parked for eternity under a hemlock. The trail makes an "S" here and descends slightly to cross Sassafras Creek on stepping stones. Upon reaching the creek's north side pass a primitive camping area on the right. The Big Snowbird Trail once again ascends, now on an east-facing slope. Trillium blooms early in this warmer micro-climate. At just over 2.8 miles arrive at the silver-blazed Sassafras Creek Trail (#65) which intersects from the left.

Sassafras Creek Trail (#65): To visit Sassafras Falls, hike the Sassafras Creek Trail and in .8 of a mile reach a point where they're heard from the trail (they're also visible when the leaves are off). Look for a slim, descending path which leads 250' through waist-high growth and over rubble to the base area.

This pristine treasure of the woods features rock that is pockmarked with potholes. The rock face splits the creek into three streams and the majority of its waters flow over the right side. Of the four waterfalls I've seen in the area, this is my favorite. It also seems to be the least visited. Return to the Big Snowbird Trail and continue upstream.

Big Falls: Continuing up the Big Snowbird Trail, now at a moderate rate, there is an abundance of in-the-trail crossties. (It seems that water from wet-weather branches acts to preserve them.) The trail crosses several wet-weather branches, one of special note, at 3.25 miles, has created a wash that affords fine views of Snowbird Creek and a small midstream island far below. Losing sight and sound of the creek, in a long right bend, the trail outlines two hollows, much like an "M." In their depths the trail undulates over rock and roots and for the moment becomes more difficult. Exiting the hollows with a left bend, at 3.6 miles the trail straightens and becomes easier. In approximately 300' look carefully for the steep access to the lower portion of Big Falls. Scramble down the slope and in 150' reach the base of Big Falls.

Big Falls is a 400'-long series of cascades over a wide rock expanse with scoured-out swirlholes. Looking upstream the scene is one of cascade after cascade, with a small waterfall topping them off.

To reach the upper portion of the cascades, return to the main trail and hike upstream approximately 450' to a barely-discernable side path leading to creek level. (Preceding this path look for a large [100' long], noticeable boulder outcrop, on the left, where the railroad bed was blasted into the side of the mountain.) The side path descends steeply for 80' through a tunnel of rhododendron to the creek bank. Once there, you must lower yourself to the bedrock viewing area of the upper tier.

The upper portion of this waterfall falls in 3' steps then makes a 10' slide over smooth bedrock into a bottomless pool. The outstanding feature here is the beautiful rock. In early spring the star-like white flowers of serviceberry are among the first to be seen streamside. As well, its red-green leaves add color to the gray woodland backdrop.

Middle Falls: Back on the main trail, continue upstream. At 3.8 miles arrive at a confusing split. The correct route veers left and ascends the sloping crest of a ridge treading in-ground steps, while the old railroad bed continues straight ahead. Descending the far side of the ridge, the trail then switchbacks down to cross Snowbird Creek on a footlog-type footbridge. Now on the north side of the creek, pass through a primitive campsite and in 110' (from the bridge, 3.9 miles into the hike) intersect the Middle Falls Trail.

The Forest Service is encouraging use of the Middle Falls Trail to access Middle and Upper Falls instead of the old route (the Big Snowbird Trail), as it is less dangerous. I prefer this route, as well, as it allows year-round access.

Middle Falls Trail (#64A): The Middle Falls Trail climbs steeply in ramp fashion, then switchbacks to gain a total of 280' in elevation ascending Mouse Knob. Now on higher ground, the trail undulates and meanders westerly. At 4.2 miles top a saddle and descend into the hollow of a small unnamed creek. In .2 of a mile the trail turns sharply left as it nears this bubbling creek. Hiking downstream, in 60' cross the creek on the remains of a logging bridge. In another 65' the trail turns sharply right and treads a rutted logging road (for a short distance). After ascending moderately, the trail levels off and undulates on the south slopes of Mouse Knob. Four and three-forths miles into the hike, atop a ridge, the trail turns abruptly right, then in 125' turns sharply left and descends the low point of a hollow. At 4.85 miles cross to the left side of a small boggy branch that rises in this hollow. At this crossing there are the remains of an old logging bridge as well. At 4.95 miles arrive at the Middle Falls Side Trail. (A sign called attention to this intersection at the time of my hike.)

Middle Falls Side Trail: Hike the Middle Falls Side Trail and in 830' arrive at the blue-blazed Big Snowbird Trail. Hike downstream for 335' and arrive at the side path to Middle Falls. Take the side path for 180' to the base area.

The fall's rock face is over 100' wide with the creek's waters occupying half of its width. The bedrock is uniformly curved at the top and the falls make a cascading plunge of 15' into a large and very deep pool.

To reach Upper Falls return to the Middle Falls Trail.

Upper Falls: Continuing towards Upper Falls the orange-blazed Middle Falls Trail bends sharply right and descends to cross a creek in approximately 100'. The trail then ascends and tops a point of land and descends once again. At just over 5 miles, the Middle Falls Trail intersects the blue-blazed Big Snowbird Trail which continues both north and south. Northbound, the trail heads towards a creek approximately 50' away. Southbound (left) it crosses Snowbird Creek on a suspension-type footbridge approximately 40' away.

Hiking north, towards Upper Falls, the trail dips and immediately crosses the aforementioned tributary of Snowbird Creek, then undulates while heading upstream along the east bank of Snowbird Creek. In approximately 700', the trail dips and crosses a small wet-weather branch then treads the old logging railroad bed once again. After treading through several wet spots and passing several fire rings, while heading northwesterly, at 5.75 miles the trail makes a gradual bend north, in harmony with the creek. At 5.8 miles the trail makes an abrupt right where the logging railroad once crossed the creek on a trestle. The trail now narrows and becomes more difficult as it undulates upstream along a rocky and root-laced slope, deeply shaded by dense rhododendron. (This slope has a few treacherous spots, with steep creekside dropoffs and jagged rock.) In .15 of a mile (5.95 miles) arrive in the vicinity of the base of Upper Falls. The trail is in the creek's flood plain here and after heavy rainfall may be under water.

Upper Falls is a shoaling waterfall, approximately 100' in length and 15' high. There is no safe frontal view as the pool is too deep. A side view of this waterfall lies 210' upstream.

To reach this viewpoint, hike uphill through the rhododendron thicket and reintersect the old logging railroad bed alongside the falls.

2. Joyce Kilmer-Citico Creek Area, Graham Co., N.C., Monroe Co., Tn.

Note: F.S. 81 may be gated. Check with the Cheoah Ranger Station located on Massey Branch Road.

Directions: From the intersection of Massey Branch Road (S.R. 1116) and S.R. 1127, drive north on 1127 (Snowbird Road, whose name soon becomes Santeetlah Road) for 7 miles to a double left turn at Santeetlah Gap. The first left is the Cherohala Skyway (N.C. 143 West), the second left is F.S. 81 (a descending paved road that soon gives way to gravel) the route to the falls. F.S. 81

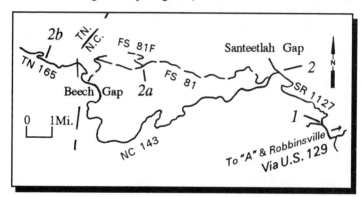

descends into the Santeetlah Creek drainage and in 1.4 miles crosses a concrete bridge. At 3.5 miles arrive at the Stewart Cabin. (Stop for a local history lesson.) Drive a total of 6.8 miles to F.S. 81F. (See The Falls on Cold Branch pg. 12 for further directions.)

To reach Fall Branch Falls, Tennessee, continue west on F.S. 81. In 2.4 miles pass F.S. 81C on the right. F.S. 81 begins a steep climb here. Four and one-tenth miles from F.S. 81F arrive at Stratton Meadows (pavement). Stay to the left and continue uphill to re-intersect N.C. 143. *Do not take the road leading under the bridge.*

Check your odometer at Hwy. 143 and drive west for 3.2 miles (1.5 miles from Beech Gap, the N.C./TN. state line) to the Fall Branch Fall's parking area and Trailhead on the right. See Fall Branch Falls pg. 12 for hiking directions.

On the way to Fall Branch check out the scenery at one of the many overlooks on N.C. 143/TN. 165.

2a. Falls on Cold Branch,
Graham County, N. Carolina

Roads: High Clearance   A "3"   30'
U.S.G.S. Quadrangle: Santeetlah Creek, N.C.
No official trail, 200', easy, (no hiking map needed)

Note: F.S. 81F is one lane and very steep. After viewing the falls drive up the mountain .3 of a mile further and use the pullout on the left as a turnaround.

Directions: Turn right onto F.S. 81F and drive .3 of a mile. Park on the left side of the road. A large boulder is located on the right side of the road at the correct location. Be very careful here. The road is narrow with just enough room for parking and another car to pass. Look to the left for the barely visible falls which are approximately 200' off the road.

Negotiate your way down the bank and wade through the waist-high growth. Look for a hole in the laurel to gain access to the creek.

This waterfall is broader than it is high. Its rock face is laced with potholes. What really caught my eye though, was the cove downstream whose boulders are covered in the greenest of mosses.

2b. Fall Branch Falls,
Monroe County, Tennessee

Roads: Graveled   A "10"   60'
U.S.G.S. Quadrangle: Big Junction, Tn.-N.C.
Trail #87, 1.3 miles, minor water crossing, difficult

I know this is a book on the Carolinas, but while we're in the area let's go sneak a peek at a Tennessee treasure.

Directions: From Beech Gap which is on the North Carolina—Tennessee line, drive west on Hwy. 165 for 1.5 miles to the parking area on the right. The trail begins at the west end of the parking area.

As you enter the woods the trail (an old roadbed) passes through knee- to waist-high growth. In 225' arrive at the trail register. Here, the Fall's Branch Trail veers left and the Jeffrey Hell Trail (#196) leads to the right.

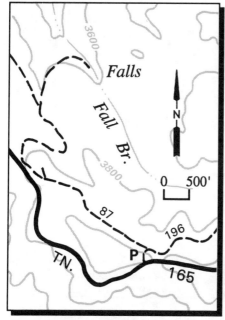

The Fall's Branch Trail parallels the north face of Sassafras Ridge for .3 of a mile then bends left. Slightly more than .4 of a mile into the hike arrive at a confusing trail on the right that leads to a small knob. Stay left here and pass through a saddle-type gap.

At the half-mile point the trail runs close to Hwy. 165 then bends right to round the mountain. Soon the trail bends left as it outlines a cove. As you exit this bend, look very carefully for a side trail on the right that leaves this roadbed. For further verification look for a large (3' in diameter) hemlock, 30' off the main trail. When I visited the falls this tree had a faded white arrow painted on it pointing the way.

Take the side trail over the rise passing by the hemlock. On the downslope you'll encounter lots of loose rock and roots galore. Three-tenths of a mile from the main trail, cross Fall Branch and pass through a big split boulder. The trail leads upstream another 300' to the base of the falls.

This waterfall falls over a showy cirque-like cliff, which is at least 250' across. It also has an adequate year-round flow which is surprising for a creek so close to the ridge line.

Map "B-C" Tapoco Area

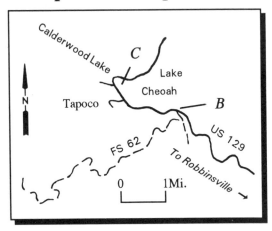

B. Wildcat Falls,
Graham Co., N.C., Monroe Co., Tn.

Roads: Graveled,   A "10" 3 tiers of equal height (10')
Map: Joyce Kilmer-Slickrock Wilderness, Trails: #41 (Big Fat
Trail), #44 (Nichols Cove), #42 (Slickrock Creek Trail)
2.75 miles, potentially deep water crossings, difficult

Note: The Slickrock Creek Trail connects with Lower Falls (see pg. 16) then eventually ends at Tapoco. Visiting both requires an overnight stay and a grand total of 12 creek crossings.

Directions: From U.S. Hwy. 129 take F.S. 62 (Big Fat Gap Road) for 7.2 miles to the parking area at Big Fat Gap.

The trail enters the woods on the west side of the parking area (behind the information board) and descends steeply into a flower-filled hollow. Every variety of trillium imaginable thrives on the moist slopes.

Winding while descending, the trail encounters a wet-weather branch at .35 of a mile where it turns sharply left. At .45 of a mile the trail crosses a rocky wet spot. This, and other soon to be encountered trickles, are the headwaters of Big Fat Branch, which will accompany us for a mile or so. At .55 of a mile cross to the north side of the wet-weather branch. The trail then turns sharply left and continues to descend along its north side. At just over .75 of a mile pass a confusing path (the old trail) leading straight ahead. The trail now turns left and dips to cross to the south side of what has become Big Fat Branch. The trail now treads an old, but well-defined roadbed and for the next half mile descends, at a lesser rate, and crosses several wet-weather branches.

At 1.25 miles the route turns sharply right and switchbacks into the creek bottom. Often within sight of the creek, the trail now more closely follows Big Fat Branch downstream while treading the old roadbed. At 1.6 miles arrive at the intersection of the Nichols Cove Trail (#44).

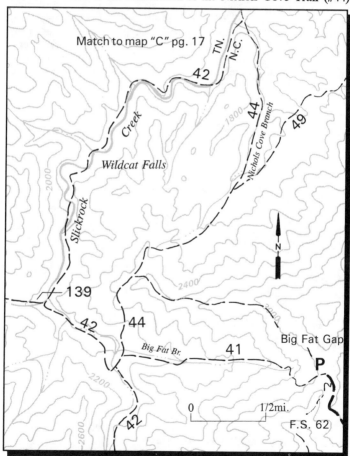

Veer left here. At 1.65 miles the Nichols Cove Trail intersects the Slickrock Creek Trail (#42) which leads both left and right. Veer right. In 200', after passing through a primitive campsite, arrive at beautiful Slickrock Creek. The trail crosses to the creek's west side here, to tread an old logging railroad bed. (Trail location may be tough here, as hikers have taken different routes to cross the creek. On my visits I found a suitable crossing 200' upstream from this prominent campsite.)

Upon crossing Slickrock Creek, immediately tread a rock outcrop then pass through an open hardwood forest. Just downstream the railroad bed is built up out of the creek's flood plain. At 2.05 miles the trail bends slightly left, away from Slickrock Creek and soon crosses a wet-weather branch. Soon treading closer to the creek, at just over 2.1 miles pass over a very narrow and slick rock outcrop which is constricted by shale cliffs on the left and the creek on the right. Just shy of 2.2 miles the trail dips to cross an unnamed creek. At 2.35 miles, in the vicinity of Big Stack Gap Branch, arrive at the intersection of the Big Stack Gap Branch Trail (#139). Approximately 50' downstream from this intersection cross to the east (North Carolina) side of Slickrock Creek. Two and sixty-five hundredths miles into the hike pass a prominent fire ring on the left. In 80' the trail dips to cross to the Tennessee side of Slickrock Creek. Upon crossing, the trail bends left while rounding a slick and tricky rock outcrop. The falls lie to the right of this outcrop. Passing alongside them, the treadway widens while descending to a full view of Wildcat Falls.

This is a very beautiful triple waterfall flowing in an "S" bend in the creek. The upper tier is distant while the lower and middle tiers are more closely stationed. The middle tier has dimpled and potholed bedrock with crisscrossing veins of quartz. The lower tier splashes into a large blue-green pool brimming with hundreds of colorful rounded stones. A small, rocky, driftwood-strewn island of sorts lies downstream. Birch and alder thrive here.

C. Lower Falls on Slickrock Creek, Graham Co., N.C., Monroe Co., Tn.

Roads: Paved,   A "4" 10'
Map: Joyce Kilmer—Slickrock Wilderness
Trail #42, 3.1 miles, water crossing, difficult

Note: This trail goes on to connect with Wildcat Falls.
This is a rugged hike over undulating and very rocky terrain. The trail looks deceptively easy on the official hiking map.

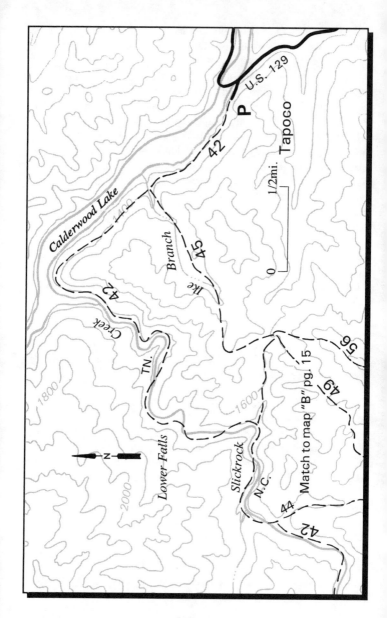

U.S. 129

P

Tapoco

42

1/2 mi.

0

Calderwood Lake

1400

45

Ike

Branch

42

Creek

T.N.

1800

1600

56

49

Match to map "B" pg. 15

Lower Falls

2000

Slickrock

N.C.

44

42

N

17

I hiked to Lower Falls in the fall and had no problem making the one creek crossing. I'm sure that winter and spring rains would raise the creek, covering the stepping stones.

Directions: Just before the U.S. 129 Bridge over Calderwood Lake look for a graveled road on the left. This leads to trail parking near a sewage treatment plant .1 of a mile ahead. Park in the pullout provided. The trailhead and information board are 200' ahead.

The trail (an old logging road) starts as a pleasant but distant shoreline hike alongside Calderwood Lake. In .5 of a mile the trail narrows to a single track. Six-tenths of a mile into the hike, after a slight ascent, arrive at the Ike Branch Trail (#45) which splits leading west. The Slickrock Trail continues closely following Calderwood Lake's shoreline. At .7 of a mile, the trail outlines the Ike Branch Cove and then crosses the creek on the first of many footbridges. As you exit the cove, the lake comes back into view. At .9 of a mile, round a rock outcrop that is girdled by a footbridge. You'll encounter three more bridged outcrops on this rugged section of the trail.

One and six-tenths miles into the hike, reach a high point with a very becoming view of Calderwood Lake to the north. The trail bends ninety degrees to the left here and crosses the wilderness boundary while entering Slickrock Creek's Cove. The trail is level for 200' then descends. At 1.75 miles a pathway leads down to Slickrock Creek. Soon, the main trail crosses a rock outcrop on a footbridge. At 1.9 miles reach the creek bottom and pass by a trail leading downstream to Calderwood Lake. Two and one-tenth miles into the hike reach a potentially confusing area. Here, a slim path leads to the creek, while the main trail goes left and uphill. At 2.2 miles the creek bends to the right. Notice the 150' high rock wall on the left. Here you'll encounter alot of windfallen trees. The creek widens and you'll soon pass a fire ring. Just ahead the trail is narrowed by a rock outcrop and a deep pool. At 2.5 miles reach a beautiful rocky area which makes for tough going. During the rainy season the trail would be in the creek here. The trail re-enters the woods and at 2.8 miles is forced to the Tennessee side of Slickrock Creek by an impassable rock outcrop. The creek is very deep here. Look slightly downstream for stepping stones to cross on. At 3 miles cross a small cascading tributary. In another .1 of a mile you'll arrive at Lower Falls.

Although the falls are not large, their surroundings make them very beautiful. Lots of rubble with clear green-tinted waters.

Franklin Area

This is North Carolina's gemstone region. Garnet, rubies, and corundum are mined here. Many area creeks show color in their sands.

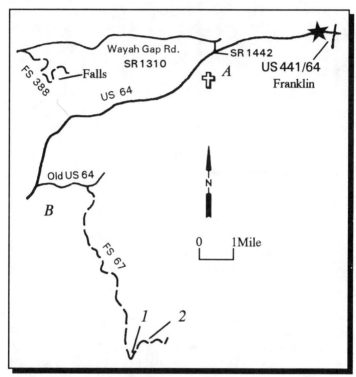

A. Rough Fork Falls, Rufus Morgan Trail, Macon County, N. Carolina

Roads: Graveled   A "5" 80'
U.S.G.S. Quadrangle: Wayah Bald, N.C.
Trail #27, .5 of a mile, water crossings, moderate-difficult

A. Directions: From the intersection of U.S. Hwys. 441 and 64 just

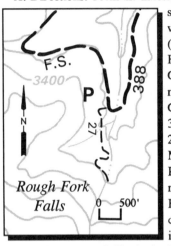

south of Franklin, N. Carolina, drive west on 64 for 3.9 miles. Turn right (north) onto S.R. 1442 (across the Hwy. from Mt. Hope Baptist Church). In approximately .1 of a mile turn left onto S.R. 1310 (Wayah Gap Road). Drive 6.5 miles to F.S. 388. Turn left (south) and drive for 2.1 miles arriving at the A. Rufus Morgan Parking Area and Trailhead. Park here. The fall's trail is on the north side of the Left Prong of Rough Fork Creek. (Don't be confused by a creekside road 100' south of the parking area, as it doesn't lead to the falls.)

Hike the steep switchbacks leading up the mountainside. In approximately .25 of a mile the trail levels out and crosses a small unnamed branch. In another .2 of mile, cross the fall's branch below a small waterfall. Continue for 300' to the base of the high falls.

In the spring you'll encounter a profusion of foam flower and lesser amounts of trillium and jack-in-the-pulpit on the trail side.

B. Directions: From the intersection of U.S. Hwys. 441 and 64 just south of Franklin, N.C., drive west on U.S. 64 for 12.2 miles to Old U.S. 64. Turn left and continue 1.9 miles to F.S. 67 on the right (sign: "Standing Indian Campground"). Take F.S. 67 to these points of interest:

1. Big Laurel Falls: 7.0 miles (pullout with sign).
2. Mooney Falls: 7.65 miles (pullout with sign).

1. Big Laurel Falls,
Macon County, N. Carolina

Roads: Graveled   A "6" 20'
Map: Southern Nantahala Wilderness and Standing Indian Basin
Trail #29, easy

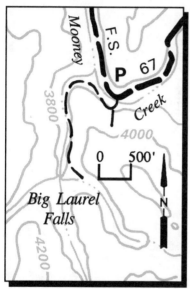

From the parking area, the trail descends and turns right. After crossing a footbridge the trail follows Mooney Creek downstream for .2 of a mile. The treadway then turns left following Big Laurel Creek upstream an additional .4 of a mile to the base of the falls.

Ease of access makes this a highly visited location.

2. Mooney Falls,
Macon County, N. Carolina

Roads/Map: See Big Laurel   A "4"
Trail #31, 5 minutes, moderate, (no hiking map needed)

Hike 200' down a steep trail that intersects the midsection of the falls.
Mooney Falls is at its best with a clear-blue sky as a backdrop. Wintertime affords the best views. Water levels are higher and the leaves being off allow a frontal view not available during other seasons.

21

Highlands Area

This area is divided into three routes with waterfalls along U.S. 64, N.C. 106, and N.C. 28 South (see text).

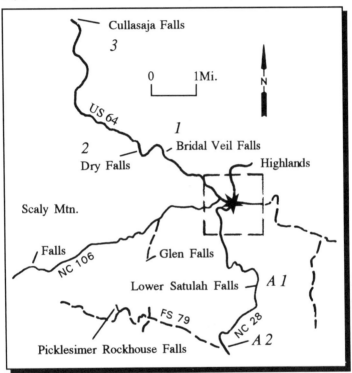

Via U.S. 64

Directions: From the intersection of U.S. Hwy. 64 and N.C. 106 in Highlands, drive west on U.S. 64 to the following points of interest. All are located on pavement and are in Macon County.

1. Bridal Veil Falls: 2.35 miles.
2. Dry Falls: 3.25 miles.
3. Cullasaja Falls: 8.9 miles.

1. Bridal Veil Falls

U.S.G.S. Quadrangle: Highlands, N.C.   A "4"
Can be seen from car

A paved semi-circular pullout on the north side of U.S. 64 leads behind the falls. Park and walk away from the falls to see its upper reaches. During the dry months this waterfall is barely a trickle.

2. Dry Falls

U.S.G.S. Quadrangle: Highlands, N.C.   A "7" 40'
Easy

A paved trail leads from the parking area for .2 of a mile to the base of the falls. Walk behind this powerful waterfall to a viewing area on the west side.

3. Cullasaja Falls

U.S.G.S. Quadrangle: Scaly Mountain, N.C.   A "7" 250'

Look for a paved pullout on the left providing a good view of this waterfall. The pullout is located in a blind curve with no room to turn around. To safely view them, you'll need to drive a mile or so more and return.

Cullasaja is a thundering giant, which falls into a deep and beautiful rocky gorge.

Easy access, high water levels, and the chance to view them under icy conditions make winter a great time to visit all three of these locations.

Via N.C. 106

Glen Falls

Roads: Graveled   A "6" multi-tiered
U.S.G.S. Quadrangle: Highlands, N.C.
Trail #8, Top: easy, Base: difficult

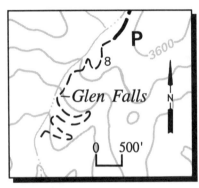

Directions: From the intersection of U.S. 64 and N.C. Hwy. 106 in Highlands, drive south on 106 for 1.8 miles. Turn left onto S.R. 1618 and in 1.1 miles arrive at the parking area and trailhead.

Hike the descending trail downstream for .3 of a mile to the overlook and top of the falls. There is a great view of the Blue Valley here. The distant mountains are located in Rabun County, Georgia.

The trail continues downstream for .4 of a mile, descending a series of switchbacks en route to the base of the upper and lower falls.

Waterfall on Scaly Mountain

U.S.G.S. Quadrangle: Scaly Mountain, N.C.   A "4"
Trail #67, 15 minutes, moderate-difficult

Note: Best seen after rainfall.
Directions: From the turnoff for Glen Falls, continue on 106 an additional 3.95 miles to the Osage Mountain Overlook. Park here.

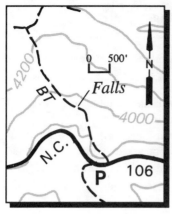

Hike the Bartram Trail north (steps on the north side of Hwy. 106) for .4 of a mile to an obscure side trail on the left (listen carefully for falling water). Take the side trail for 100' to a very pretty 15' waterfall. If you cross a substantial (year-round) creek, you've gone too far.

Via N.C. 28 South

Directions: From the intersection of N.C. Hwy. 28 South and U.S. 64 in Highlands, drive south on 28 to the following points of interest:

A1. The Lower Satulah Falls Overlook: 3.7 miles.
A2. S.R. 1618/F.S. 79 access to Picklesimer Rockhouse Falls: 6.1 miles.

A1. Lower Satulah Falls

This waterfall is seen from an overlook on the west side of Hwy. 28. Look west approximately 1500' for this high and slim beauty. Winter offers the best views and water levels. I stopped here on a summer day and couldn't see them for the heavy vegetation and lack of water.

A2. Pickleslimer Rockhouse Falls

Roads: Graveled   An "8" 35'
U.S.G.S. Quadrangles: Highlands, Scaly Mtn., N.C., in their margins
.6 of a mile, shallow water crossings, moderate

Note: This waterfall is high on the slopes of Little Scaly Mtn. and is therefore best seen after adequate rainfall.

Directions: From Hwy. 28 turn right (west) onto S.R. 1618/ F.S. 79 and drive 4.4 miles to an unmarked Forest Service road on the right. This road is neither numbered on maps, or in the field. Park on the *left* side of F.S. 79 in the pullout provided, so as to not block the gate.

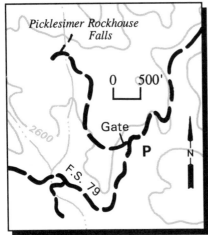

Hike the unmarked logging road and in 200' pass the gate. In .1 of a mile, after having crested the ridge line, the road bends right and continues its gradual ascent. The road then tops out and descends as you enter an area of recent logging activity. Next, you'll pass through a wildlife opening. As you reach the northwest edge of this opening (slightly more than .4 of a mile of into the hike) cross the fall's branch. In 30' look for a slim path which enters the thicket and leads upstream. Take this path for .1 of a mile to the base of the falls.

I visited this location shortly after rainfall and during a cold spell that made it especially beautiful. The cliff was decorated with icicles, some of which were four feet long. Aside from that, the alcove has some of the most ornately grained rock that I've seen. Please wait for adequate rainfall to see this waterfall—you'll surely not be disappointed.

Cashiers—Sapphire Area

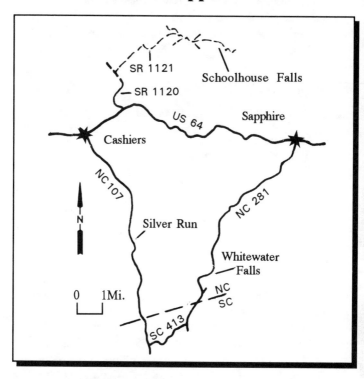

SR 1121

Schoolhouse Falls

SR 1120

US 64

Sapphire

Cashiers

NC 107

Silver Run

NC 281

N

Whitewater
Falls

0   1Mi.

NC
SC

SC 413

Silver Run Falls,
Jackson County, N. Carolina

Roads: Paved   An "8" 25'
U.S.G.S. Quadrangle: Cashiers, N.C.
.2 of a mile, 5 minutes, easy, (no hiking map needed)

Note: Bring a hiking stick to help balance yourself on the log serving as a footbridge.

Directions: From the intersection of U.S. 64 and N.C. 107 in Cashiers, drive south on 107 for 4.1 miles. Park at the second graveled pullout on the left. (A utility pole is located at the correct pullout.) The trail enters the woods just south of the pole.

Hike .1 of a mile and then use the log to cross a 10' wide creek. Once across, the trail turns to the right and continues a short distance downstream to the base of the falls. This is a very pretty waterfall with a large blue-green plunge pool.

Schoolhouse Falls, Panthertown Valley, Jackson County, N. Carolina

Roads: Graveled   A   "4"   15'
U.S.G.S. Quadrangle: Big Ridge, N.C.
2.4 miles, water crossings, moderate-difficult

Directions: From the intersection of U.S. 64 and N.C. Hwy. 107 in Cashiers, drive east on U.S. 64 for 2 miles to Cedar Creek Road (S.R. 1120). Turn left (north) and drive 2.3 miles to Breedlove Road (S.R. 1121). Turn right and travel 3.8 miles to the parking area and gate.

From the gate the roadbed leading into Panthertown Valley descends steeply. In approximately 300' sign up at the trail register. The roadbed serving as our trail soon levels then turns uphill while bending right. At .3 of a mile pass through a saddle atop Salt Rock. From an opening, view the beautiful plutonic domes of Big and Little Green mountains to the east and Blackrock Mtn. to the northeast. (The plutonic domes of the Panthertown Valley consist of Granitoid Gneiss.) Schoolhouse Falls lie just beyond Little Green Mtn.

The trail begins to descend once again. Rock exposures and small trees in this area are covered heavily in lichens. At .6 of a mile pass a road leading to the right. (This leads to the falls on Frolictown Creek which will be visited later.*) The trail now straightens out and for the moment levels somewhat. At .8 of a mile the road makes a right bend and descends more steeply. At .85 of a mile arrive at a four-way intersection. (The route to the right leads to Granny Burrells Falls, which will be visited later, as well.**) The route to Schoolhouse Falls continues straight ahead and the roadbed narrows to a wide, single track. At .95 of a mile the treadway levels

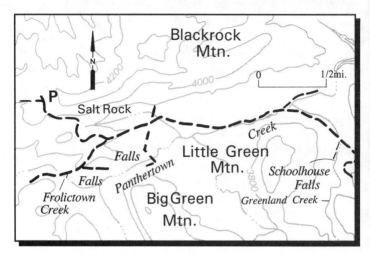

amongst white pine, hemlock, and rhododendron. A small branch
flows alongside the old roadbed here. Now in the valley floor and
undulating, at 1.4 miles the roadbed widens as it joins Panthertown
Creek. After crossing a small tributary branch, the next landmark
shown on the quadrangle is a large pool (known as Sandbar Pool,
1.7 miles) with a sliding rock on its upper end and a plywood
fisherman's cabin on the banks of its lower end. (Look for a piped
spring, on the left, just prior to the cabin.) The roadbed makes a left
and right jog to circumvent the pool. After being somewhat open,
pass under a canopy of white pine. Soon thereafter (1.85 miles) the
road forks. Take the right fork which immediately crosses
Panthertown Creek on an old wooden auto bridge. (This bridge is
in an advanced state of decline, so don't count on it still being intact.)
Of special note in this vicinity is the occurrence of Fraser fir.

As we enter the drainage of Greenland Creek, the roadbed
passes the rhododendron-covered slopes of Little Green Mtn. and
through many bogs. At 2.25 miles (50' short of another dilapidated
auto bridge, this one spanning Greenland Creek) look for a slim path
leaving the roadbed and leading right. This path meanders upstream for .15 of a mile to Schoolhouse Falls.

A large sandbar preceeds the falls. Golf ball to softball-sized gneiss gravel is strewn about its sands. The plunge pool is approximately 80' wide and extends 60' out from the falls. Full of rock and clear, the pool shimmers a sunlit golden green. Alder, birch, and hemlock reside on its sandbars. The falls are 15' high, total, consisting of a 10' drop preceeded by a 5' cascade. As well, they are approximately 15' wide during average flow.

They are best photographed on an overcast day in the growing season. Early morning or late afternoon when the sun is low, also works well. In winter, lens flare is a problem here as the sun sweeps low across the sky directly behind the falls.

*Frolictown Falls: From the main trail, the side trail (an old roadbed) leads uphill (at an easy to moderate rate) and in 600' passes the site of an old homestead. Soon topping out, the trail descends at a moderate rate and passes an old road that intersects from the left. At .45 of a mile arrive at a ford of Frolictown Creek. Backtrack 30' and descend the steep slope to access the base of the falls.

**Granny Burrells Falls: Leaving the main trail with a compass bearing of S 20° W, the road to Granny Burrells Falls makes a bend right traveling level for approximately 125'. With a slight descent the roadbed straightens and at 350' bends left. At .1 of a mile look for a brick barbecue and fire ring approximately 75' to the trail's left. The route now meanders through a level area, then at .15 of a mile enters an opening with Big Green Mtn. looming to the south. At the quarter-mile point arrive alongside Panthertown Creek. The creek flows straight towards the viewer then makes a sharp bend east (a very scenic setting). In 150' cross an old wooden auto bridge over Panthertown Creek. The fall's rushing waters can be heard in this vicinity, upstream. At .3 of a mile, with two water-filled depressions straight ahead, look for a slim path leading right. Take this side path and soon tread an old roadbed leading alongside Panthertown Creek. The path soon narrows into a well-defined single-lane treadway. At .4 of a mile the path is forced onto the creek's bedrock. The falls lie 100' upstream.

(This could be a hazardous area in the wintertime because of ground water seeping, then freezing on the bedrock.) The fall's rock face is approximately 40' wide. Panthertown Creek enters the scene through a shallow U-shaped bedrock channel, then flows over rounded bedrock, shoaling as a 15'-high fall. A small, shallow pool lies at its base. Laurel and rhododendron grow on its flanks. Small white pines form the backdrop. Look for a drill bit atop the falls on the right.

The creek exits the pool and shoals over banded gneiss for approximately 100', slipping into a much larger pool. Sandbars enhance the beauty of the pool's woodland setting.

For more detailed information on the geology and other trails in this area, purchase a copy of *A Guide's Guide to Panthertown Valley, by Burt Kornegay*. This handy map/brochure may be purchased from Slickrock Expeditions, Inc., P.O. Box 1214, Cullowhee, N.C., 28723.

Whitewater Falls—Falls on Corbin Creek, Transylvania County, N. Carolina

Roads: Paved   Whitewater An "8", easy to viewpoint
Corbin Creek A "6" 70', water crossings, difficult
U.S.G.S. Quadrangle: Cashiers, N.C., U.S. Fee Area

Note: The trails above Whitewater Falls leading to its base are informal and dangerous. The best views are from the overlooks at the end of the paved trail.

Directions: From the intersection of U.S. 64 and N.C. 281/F.S. 1171, in the community of Sapphire, drive south on 281 for 8.6 miles to a left turn which leads .2 of a mile to the Whitewater Fall's Parking Area.

Alternate directions: From the intersection of U.S. 64 and N.C. Hwy. 107 in Cashiers, drive south on 107 for 9.3 miles to *South Carolina* Hwy. 413/F.S. 106 (sign: Whitewater Falls). Turn left and drive 2.2 miles to Hwy. 281/F.S. 1171 (stop sign). Turn left and continue 1.15 miles to a right turn which leads to the parking area .2 of a mile away.

At 411', Whitewater Falls is thought to be the highest waterfall in the eastern U.S. To view them, walk .2 of a mile up a paved trail

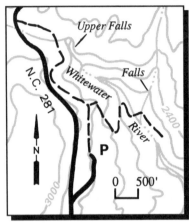

to the overlook. At the overlook, an old roadbed to the left leads to the top of the falls .3 of a mile away, then continues to Hwy. 281/F.S. 1171 upstream from the falls (a 1 mile hike total). The trail to the right leads down to another overlook framed by Carolina hemlock.

Corbin Creek

The Foothills Hiking Trail continues steeply down from this point to the Whitewater River. If possible, ask if a footbridge crossing the river is in place before you commit yourself to hiking into the gorge.

When you reach the gorge bottom, the Foothills Trail crosses the Whitewater River. A massive log with a handrail served as a footbridge here until washed away. Hopefully you'll find the bridge replaced. (During periods of high water, wading the river could be dangerous.) A short distance away is a footbridge over Corbin Creek. Upstream just out of view is a beautiful waterfall on Corbin Creek.

Lake Toxaway Area

Directions: From the intersection of U.S. Hwy. 64 and N.C. 281 *North,* just east of the Lake Toxaway Dam, drive north on 281 for 1.45 miles to Slick Fisher Road (S.R. 1306). Turn left and drive 4.55 miles and re-intersect Hwy. 281 near the now vacant Big Pisgah Church. As you turn left (north) onto Hwy. 281 (a graveled road) check your mileage and travel the following distances to:

1. The parking area for Dismal Falls[1] : .35 of a mile.

2. F.S. 5070, access to Mill Branch[1] : 1.1 miles.

3. Owens Gap: 2.3 miles.

[1] These waterfalls are located in the Pisgah N. F. They are listed here because of their close proximity to points of interest in the Nantahala N. F.

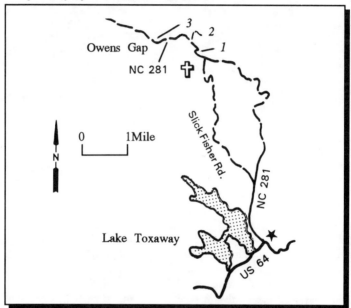

1. Unnamed Waterfall, Dismal Falls, Transylvania County, N. Carolina

Roads: Graveled   A "3" 35' & A "10" 60' respectively
U.S.G.S. Quadrangle: Lake Toxaway, N.C.
1.7 miles, no official trail, water crossings, difficult

Note: Allow at least one-half day.

Park on the east shoulder of the road in the space provided. Directly across the road (west) is a gated logging road that serves as the trail.

Hike the logging road. In .2 of a mile, pass through the first of three wildlife openings. Continue a total of .5 of a mile to an open stand of white pine, near the eastern end of the *second* wildlife opening. Leave the logging road here on a path which leads north and passes through a primitive campground. Seven hundred feet from the logging road is a small, but very nice 35', three-tier waterfall.

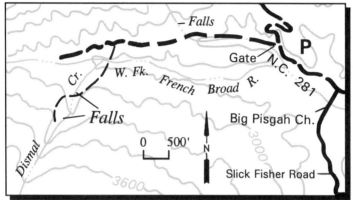

Return to the logging road and continue the hike westward. In approximately .2 of a mile, pass through the third wildlife opening. Three-tenths of a mile ahead, you'll pass under power lines. Shortly, you'll encounter a trail on the left. Pay it no attention. Continue for an additional .2 of a mile (1.2 miles from the gate) to an open stand of white pine. Walk south through the pines for 300' and rock-hop across the West Fork of the French Broad River (more like a creek than river). After passing through the streamside vegetation, you'll encounter a somewhat open stand of small hardwoods with waist-high underbrush. Hike southwesterly (away from the river) ascending the cove that houses Dismal Creek. Soon you'll hear the lower falls. Hike to their base and take a break while drinking in the sights.

The lower falls are a beauty, spilling from ledge to ledge. They are quite noisy for their size.

With the easy part behind us, when you're rested we'll carry on.

To reach Dismal Falls, cross the lower falls at their base and climb the steep bank on the west side. About a 100' away intersect an old overgrown logging road. (All that remains of this road is a swale and gulley.) Hike this steep logging road upstream for .3 of a mile. Look to the left for a glimpse of the falls or the rock alcove that houses them. Wade through the rhododendron thicket down to the creek. Hike the creek upstream to the base area of this pristine jewel of nature.

There is nothing dismal about it. Even the somewhat arduous hike is an adventure.

Dismal Falls has a sheer but delicate drop of about 60' from a massive rock ledge. The shallow pool at its base is flanked by large hardwoods as well as hemlock.

2. Unnamed Branch—Mill Branch, Transylvania County, N. Carolina

Roads: Graveled A "3" & A "2"
U.S.G.S. Quadrangle: Lake Toxaway, N.C.
.2 and .5 of a mile respectively, easy

Park at the pullout located here. The hike begins at the gate. Hike F.S. 5070 for .2 of a mile to a small but very pretty wet-

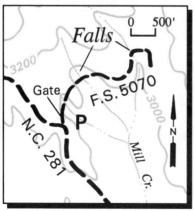

weather waterfall on the left. During the growing seasons this waterfall is obscured from view. The left side of the creek offers the best access. A careful wade through the briars and other waist-high growth is necessary to see them close-up.

Continue east on 5070 for an additional .3 of a mile to a small cascade seen from the road.

3. Owens Gap (as above).

Pisgah National Forest

The Pisgah National Forest is comprised of 495,000 acres in

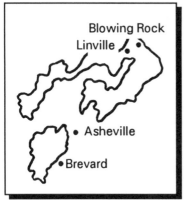

western North Carolina. The name "Pisgah" was taken from the Biblical mountain from which Moses saw the promised land. Legend has it that in 1776 Rev. James Hall, a Presbyterian minister, named the mountain while in the region fighting the Cherokee. Upon viewing the French Broad River Valley from atop what is now known as Mount Pisgah, he was reminded of the promised land which Moses had seen from the mountain bearing the same name.

The Pisgah National Forest is where scientific forestry was first practiced in America. In 1889 George W. Vanderbilt began purchasing land for his country estate "Biltmore House." Mr. Vanderbilt expanded his holdings to include Mount Pisgah. He envisioned an estate which perpetuated itself from the sale of forest products raised in "Pisgah Forest." Mr. Vanderbilt chose forestry expert Gifford Pinchot to manage this endeavor. In 1895 Dr. Carl Schenck replaced Mr. Pinchot who had gone on to be the first head of the U.S. Forest Service. Dr. Schenck started the Biltmore Forest School in 1898 to teach modern forestry techniques. The school graduated 367 students before ceasing operations in 1914.

In 1968 Congress passed the "Cradle of Forestry in America Act" which set aside 6400 acres to commemorate forest conservation in America. A visitor center is located north of Sliding Rock on U.S. 276 (see pages 46 and 61). Here also, you'll find the restored schoolhouse and living quarters of the Biltmore Forest School, as well as an old sawmill and a narrow-gauge locomotive which was used to haul logs out of the mountain's hollows.

The Land of Waterfalls
Transylvania County, N. Carolina

Seventy inches of annual rainfall and some pretty hefty mountainsides make this area a "waterfall walkers paradise." With over 200 waterfalls (many on private property), Transylvania County touts itself as "The Land of Waterfalls." Looking Glass and Whitewater Falls are the centerpieces, with their great beauty and easy accessibility. Both are heavily visited.

For those of you who are willing to travel on graveled or dirt roads and endure hikes of varying difficulty, there are ample rewards in the area too. Courthouse and Dismal Falls, both knockouts, require hikes at the ability extremes. The former—easy, the latter—somewhat ardous. In most cases when there are crowds at the "popular spots" you can visit the "lesser knowns" in peace and relative solitude.

The waterfalls in the text of pages 38 through 61 unless otherwise noted are located in Transylvania County.

Rosman—Beech Gap Area

Directions: From the intersection of U.S. Hwy. 64 and N.C. 215 near Rosman, N. Carolina, drive north on 215 to the following points of interest:

1. F.S. 140, access to the falls on the N. Fork of the French Broad River (a) the Falls on Chestnut Creek, (b) Courthouse Falls, and (c) the Upper Falls on Courthouse Creek: 10.55 miles.
2. F.S. 4663, access to Dill Falls[2] : 14.55 miles.
3. The Blue Ridge Parkway at Beech Gap: 17.15 miles.
4. The parking area for Wildcat Falls: 17.95 miles.

[2] Dill Falls is located in the Nantahala N. F., because of its close proximity to the Pisgah N. F. it is listed here.

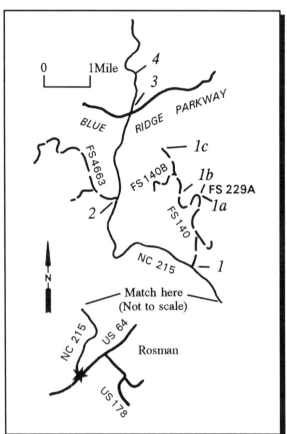

1a. Falls on Chestnut Creek

Roads: Graveled/High Clearance   A "4" 20'
U.S.G.S. Quadrangle: Sam Knob, N.C.
20 minutes, water crossing, difficult

Directions: Turn right (north) onto F.S. 140 and drive 2.7 miles to F.S. 229A (Kiesee Creek Road) on the right. Park here.

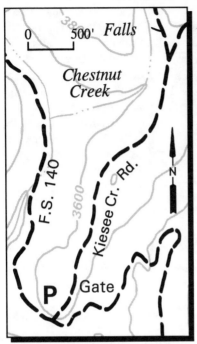

Hike Kiesee Creek Road for .6 of a mile. Where the road forks, go left. Pace off 600' from this split and listen for the falls. Scramble down the hill and intersect the creek 150' away. Hike the creek upstream approximately 100' to the fall's area.

1b. Courthouse Falls

Roads: Graveled A "10 + "
U.S.G.S. Quadrangle: Sam Knob, N.C.
Trail #'s 129/130, .3 of a mile, easy-moderate, (map next pg.)

Note: This trail has wet spots even in the dry season.

This beautiful waterfall resides in a dream-like setting and is one that I keep coming back to, time after time. There is so much beauty here that it escapes being captured on one single frame of film or in a single visit. If you miss all the rest of the waterfalls described in this book, please *do* see this one.

Directions: See the directions to the Falls on Chestnut Creek and continue north on F.S. 140 for .4 of a mile to the pullouts on the north side of the bridge. Park here. The Summey Cove Trail begins

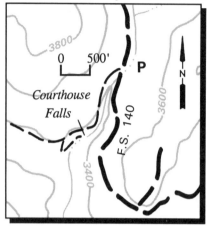

on the downstream side of the bridge.

Hike .3 of a mile downstream passing by the very audible falls. Look carefully for a slim trail on the left descending into the alcove. This trail may have a sign announcing the falls. (The Summey Cove Trail continues straight ahead leading to Hwy. 215 which is another 1.9 miles away.) Hike this side trail for 300'

to the base of the falls. On your approach you'll understand why I often visit this area.

Courthouse Creek flows through a "V" in the rock face, slides down a chute and then splashes into a very deep pool. Large hardwoods create a canopy which deeply shades the alcove, giving the plunge pool an indigo color. The rock wall on the left weeps nutrients to dozens of aquatic plants. Mosses and lichens adorn the wall on the right.

1c. Upper Falls On Courthouse Creek

Roads: Graveled   A "2" 20' & 8' respectively
U.S.G.S. Quadrangle: Sam Knob, N.C., easy

Directions: See directions to Courthouse Falls and continue north on F.S. 140 for .2 of a mile and arrive at a point where F.S. 140B, on the left, and F.S. 140 which continues on the right, are gated. Park here. Hike F.S. 140 which soon parallels Courthouse

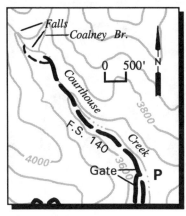

Creek and in .7 of a mile arrive at the end of the road. Continue upstream approximately 300' to a shoaling waterfall on Courthouse Creek (on the left) just upstream from its confluence with Coalney Branch. There are other falls just upstream. To reach them, return to the road's end. Look for a path which leads uphill (west) and into the woods. Hike this path for 300' to the small but very scenic upper falls.

2. Dill Falls,
Jackson County, N. Carolina

Roads: High Clearance*   A "5"
U.S.G.S. Quadrangle: Sam Knob, N.C.
.2 of a mile, 10 minutes, moderate, (map next pg.)

Directions: From the intersection of N.C. Hwy. 215 and F.S. 4663, near Cold Spring Gap, take F.S. 4663 (which leads west, passing private land) for 1.9 miles. Where F.S. 4663 starts steeply up the mountainside, look for an unimproved logging road on the left. Drive the unimproved logging road for .6 of a mile. (*This road may have deep mudholes near its end, but is generally in good condition. If carefully driven, most automobiles could negotiate this road.) As you enter a clearing (the site of recent logging activity), look to the right for a road that crosses several jeep blocking mounds while leading uphill. Park here. This road serves as the trail to the falls.

Cross the jeep blocking mounds and hike the steep road (which soon levels out) for slightly less than .2 of a mile. The falls are on the left.

41

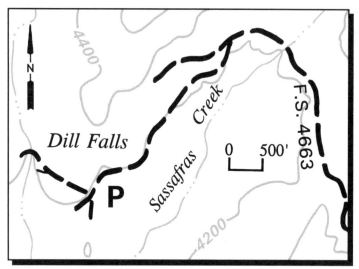

Make your way downhill through the waist-deep underbrush to the base area approximately 100' away.

3. The Blue Ridge Parkway (as above).

4. Wildcat Falls,
Haywood County, N. Carolina

Roads: Paved   A "3" 60'
U.S.G.S. Quadrangle: Sam Knob, N.C.
Trail #440, .7 of a mile, 20 minutes, easy-moderate

Note: Best seen after rainfall.

Directions: From the intersection of N.C. Hwy. 215 and the Blue Ridge Parkway, drive north on 215 for .8 of a mile to a small parking area on the right. (This parking area is somewhat obscured, as it is below road level.) Park here.

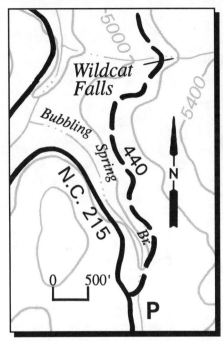

Hike the Sam Knob Trail which leads immediately across Bubbling Spring Branch (a rather large creek for one so close to the ridge). The trail (an old roadbed) then turns north and starts its rocky climb, gaining approximately 160' in elevation on its way to the falls.

A concrete bridge just below the falls provides an open viewing area.

43

Brevard West

Cathey's Creek Falls

Roads: Graveled   A "5"
U.S.G.S. Quadrangle: Rosman, N.C.
5 minutes, moderate, (no hiking map needed)

Directions: From the intersection of U.S. Hwy. 64 and U.S. 276 *South* in downtown Brevard, drive west on U.S. 64 for 3.45 miles to Cathey's Creek Road (S.R. 1401, sign: Kuykendall Group

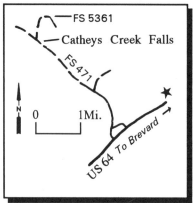

Camp). Turn right (north) and in 50' turn left onto Selica Road (S.R. 1338). In 1.1 miles pass the Brevard water treatment plant on the left. The road soon enters the Pisgah National Forest where it is designated F.S. 471. After traveling approximately 2.5 miles, F.S. 471 switchbacks to climb King Mountain. Continue for a total of 3.2 miles to an easily missed, single-vehicle pullout on the right. (The power line crosses the road here.) Park and look carefully for a faint bushwacked path on the right.

Hike this descending path for 300' as it leads upstream to the base area. Once there, carefully descend the bank to creek level where the falls come into full view.

The prelude to the falls is visible from a bridge that crosses Cathey's Creek. To reach the bridge, continue north on 471 for approximately .1 of a mile.

Brevard—Mt. Pisgah Area

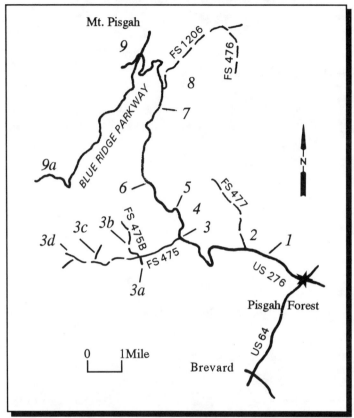

Directions: This route begins 3.5 miles east of Brevard, where U.S. Hwy. 64 and U.S. 276 *North* intersect near the community of Pisgah Forest. Drive north on U.S. 276 to the following points of interest:

1. The Pisgah Ranger Station: 1.6 miles.
2. F.S. 477, access to the Falls on Henry Branch: 2.3 miles.
3. F.S. 475, access to the falls in the Davidson River Drainage: 5.4 miles. Take F.S. 475 the following distances to:

3a. The State Fish Hatchery, access to the Falls on Cedar Rock and Grogan Creeks: 1.4 miles.

3b. F.S. 475B, access to Slick Rock Falls: 1.5 miles.

3c. F.S. 809, access to Cove Creek Falls: 3.25 miles.

3d. F.S. 137, access to Jackson Falls: 3.95 miles.

4. Looking Glass Falls: 5.7 miles.

5. Parking and trailhead for Moore Cove Falls: 6.8 miles.

6. Sliding Rock: 8.0 miles.

7. The Cradle of Forestry in America Visitor Center: 11.35 miles.

8. F.S. 1206 (Yellow Gap Road), access to the High Falls on the South Fork, Mills River: 11.95 miles.

9. The intersection of U.S. 276 and the Blue Ridge Parkway south of Mt. Pisgah: 15.3 miles. Drive west on the parkway to:

9a. The Graveyard Fields' Parking Area, access to Yellowstone Falls: 7.1 miles.

1. The Pisgah Ranger Station (as above).

2. Twin Falls of Henry Branch

Roads: Graveled A "7" 60'
U.S.G.S. Quadrangle: Shining Rock, N.C.
Trails (see text), 2.1 miles, water crossings, easy-moderate

Directions: From U.S. 276, take F.S. 477 for 2.6 miles to the Avery Creek Parking Area and Trailhead which is on the right.

Hike the yellow and blue-blazed Avery Creek Trail for .9 of a mile. There you'll intersect the blue-blazed Lower Avery Creek Trail. Take the Lower Avery Creek Trail (#327) north (upstream) for .1 of a mile (passing the horse ford) and arrive at the orange-blazed Buckhorn Gap Trail (#103). Several trees have double blue blazes announcing this intersection.

Hike east on the Buckhorn Gap Trail which now crosses Avery Creek on a footbridge. Once across the creek notice the double orange blazes denoting a potentially confusing left turn in the trail. The Buckhorn Gap Trail now follows Henry Branch upstream

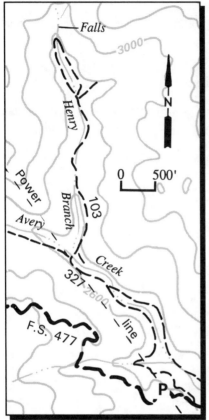

(north) making numerous creek crossings while ascending the cove.

One and one-half miles into the hike, the trail turns sharply left, then downhill to cross Henry Branch on a footbridge. Once across, notice how moss has covered old railroad ties. The trail now follows an old logging railroad bed.

At 1.7 miles the Buckhorn Gap Trail is intersected by the blue-blazed Twin Falls Loop Trail, which is on the left. Hike the Twin Falls Loop (stay on the left portion of the loop as the right portion is overgrown) and at the 2 mile point pass a small wet-weather waterfall up the cove on the left. In another .1 of a mile arrive at an area where the Falls on Henry Branch, on the left, and the unnamed branch, on the right, can be seen. The trail then crosses the base of the Falls on Henry Branch en route to the falls on the unnamed branch.

Although this is a loop trail, it is very hard to discern after passing the falls on the unnamed branch. I suggest backtracking your way out.

3. F.S. 475 (as above).

3a. Falls on Cedar Rock and Grogan Creeks

Roads: Paved   A "10" & A "4"
U.S.G.S. Quadrangle: Shining Rock, N.C., water crossing
Trail #'s 120 & 123, 25 minutes & 1 hour respectively, moderate

Directions: Enter the fish hatchery parking area. Park at the information board near the visitor center, which is .1 of a mile away. The orange-blazed Cat Gap Trail (#120) begins just across the bridge, 350' south of the information board. This trail leads to the falls.

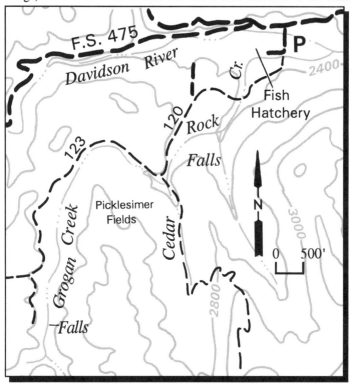

Enter the woods and in .2 of a mile cross a small unnamed branch. At .3 of a mile, cross Cedar Rock Creek on a footbridge. After crossing a road, the trail starts uphill then intersects and treads upon an old logging road in a southerly direction. Continue another .5 of a mile, while gaining over 200' in elevation, to a creekside camping area on the left.

When you arrive at the camping area, notice the small shoaling waterfall located upstream.

To reach the lower falls, look downstream and take a path angling to the left (away from the creek) that gently descends the west side of the fall's cliff. At the bottom, turn back towards the creek and walk approximately 200' to the base of the falls.

This waterfall has some of the greenest moss-covered rock that I've encountered. On a hot summer day pull up a rock and savor the natural air-conditioning as you enjoy its grace.

Return to the Cat Gap Trail and continue upstream 200' to intersect the blue-blazed Butter Gap Trail (#123). Take the Butter Gap Trail west following Grogan Creek upstream through the Picklesimer Fields. Soon the trail turns south and passes the Long Branch Trail which intersects in .6 of a mile. Continue another .4 of a mile to the Falls on Grogan Creek.

Scramble downhill to observe the falls from its base.

3b. Slick Rock Falls

Roads: Graveled   A "3" 15', (no hiking map needed)
U.S.G.S. Quadrangle: Shining Rock, N.C.

Note: Best seen after rainfall.
Directions: Turn right (north) onto F.S. 475B and drive 1.15 miles to a roadside viewing area. The falls are approximately 200' up the cove.

3c. Cove Creek Falls

Roads: Graveled   A "5" 50'
U.S.G.S. Quadrangle: Shining Rock, N.C.
Trail #361, 1.2 miles, moderate

At this location you'll find the parking area on the left (south) side of F.S. 475. The route to the falls initially treads the gated (F.S. 809) on the north side of F.S. 475. This road leads to the Cove Creek group campground and only campers are allowed to drive it.

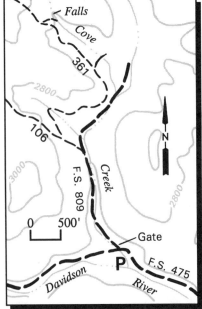

From the gate, hike the graveled and ascending F.S. 809 (up Cove Creek). In 400' the road fords the creek, while the trail veers right to cross it on a footbridge. Road and trail soon rejoin. Four tenths of a mile up the road, just before arriving at the campground, look for the Caney Bottom Loop Trail on the left (west) side of the road.

The blue-blazed Caney Bottom Loop Trail initially parallels a small unnamed creek and in 370' turns right to cross that creek (the Farlow Gap Trail [#106] continues straight ahead). Skirting the northwest side of the campground, at .55 of a mile pass through a small hollow and soon thereafter tread an old roadbed. With a long left bend, enter the hollow of Cove Creek. At .75 of a mile the blue-blazed Caney Bottom Loop Trail veers off to the right, while the unmarked fall's trail continues straight (double blue blazes call attention to this split, [there are occasional blue blazes further up the fall's trail]). At just over a mile, while exiting a hollow, the now audible falls resonate through the woods. As the trail closely encounters Cove Creek (1.15 miles), arrive at the steeply descending side trail leading .1 of a mile to the base of the falls.

3d. Jackson Falls

Roads: Graveled A "5" 60'+
U.S.G.S. Quadrangle: Shining Rock, N.C.
.5 of a mile, 10 minutes, easy-moderate

At this location you'll find a small parking area on the right. Park here. The hike begins at the gated road.

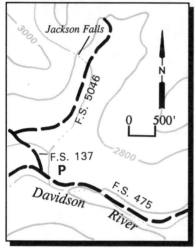

Hike the road (shown on the quadrangle as F.S. 137) northwesterly crossing the Davidson River on a concrete bridge. Six hundred and fifty feet from the gate, veer right onto F.S. 5046. Hike this ascending road for .4 of a mile to a point where the falls come into full view.

Here you'll find a huge rock exposure littered with boulders below. Winter is my favorite time to visit. The leaves are off and allow the sun to work its magic on this south-facing cliff. Despite its easy access and great beauty, you'll find no crowds here.

4. Looking Glass Falls

Roads: Paved A "10" 60', (no hiking map needed)
U.S.G.S. Quadrangle: Shining Rock, N.C., easy

This is possibly the most popular waterfall in the Brevard Area. On summer days and during the leaf season you'll have to jockey just to get a parking place. None the less this is a great beauty with lots of water in all seasons. It is also a welcome relief when nursing blistered tootsies.

The falls may be seen from an overlook adjacent to the parking area. For a much better view take the stone stairway 150' down to creek level.

Despite being next to the highway, this is a very scenic spot with high rock walls and a large pool. It needs our help though. Unappreciative visitors can't seem to hit the trash cans. The Forest Service doesn't have the personnel to police the area at all times— please help them in their efforts. I've adopted the old scouting motto "leave these sites as I found them, but if they've been trashed, in better shape than they were found."

5. Moore Cove Falls

Roads: Paved   A "5"
U.S.G.S. Quadrangle: Shining Rock, N.C.
Trail #318, .7 of a mile, 20 minutes, easy-moderate

Note: Don't be deceived by the initial steepness of this trail. It becomes easier after the first .2 of a mile.

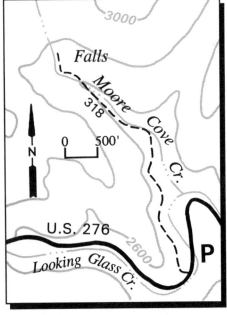

At this location there is a large parking area on the right shoulder of U.S. 276. Park here. The trail begins at the northwest corner of the stone highway bridge that crosses Looking Glass Creek.

From the bridge, the yellow-blazed trail ascends, rounds the mountain's base, then descends back to creek level. The trail now starts its gradual climb up the cove alongside Moore Cove Creek. At approximately .6 of a mile, the trail steepens a bit as it

Middle Falls, Snowbird Creek

Courthouse Falls

Falls on Cedar Rock Creek

Roaring Fork Falls

Crabtree Falls

Whitewater Falls

Falls on Yellow Branch

Lee Falls

rounds a bend to the right, whereupon the falls come into view.

This waterfall is very scenic, plunging an unbroken 60' from a massive rock ledge. A trail leads behind this thin veil-like waterfall to a vantage point on the west side.

6. Sliding Rock (as above).

7. The Cradle of Forestry in America (as above).

8. High Falls on the South Fork, Mills River

Roads: Graveled   A "4" 15'
U.S.G.S. Quadrangle: Pisgah Forest, N.C.
Trail #133, 2 miles, water crossing (potentially deep and
dangerous after periods of rain , see below*), moderate

Directions: From U.S. 276, turn right (east) onto Yellow Gap

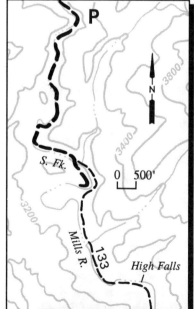

Road (F.S. 1206) and drive 3.35 miles to Wolf Ford Road (F.S. 476, a.k.a. South Mills River Road). Turn right (south) and drive 1.35 miles to a small parking area where the road is gated. Park here.

Hike the South Mills River Trail (gated logging road), which is white blazed. This is a very easy, but sometimes rocky stretch of trail following alongside the fast flowing South Fork, Mills River. In slightly less than 1 mile the road veers right and crosses a concrete bridge, while the unmaintained and unblazed trail to the falls continues dead ahead.

The trail is fairly rugged from here on, undulating over rocky and root-laced terrain with occasional windfalls.

One and six-tenths miles into the hike you'll arrive at a primitive camping area. Here, the river bends sharply left. *Continue downstream approximately 750' and ford the river. After crossing, continue another .2 of a mile on this sometimes muddy stretch of the trail to the fall's area.

9. The Blue Ridge Parkway (as above).

9a. Yellowstone Falls, (Graveyard Fields Loop Trail) MP. 418.8 Blue Ridge Parkway, Haywood County, N. Carolina

Roads: Paved
U.S.G.S. Quadrangle: Shining Rock, N.C.
Trail #358, moderate

The area around Yellowstone Falls was scorched by fire in 1925 and again in 1942. The 1925 fire was started by sparks from a steam locomotive and consumed 35,000 acres of timberland. Left behind were charred tree trunks that resembled hundreds of headstones—thus the name "Graveyard Fields."

The 1942 fire was caused by arson. Although there is plenty of greenery now, there are no large trees to speak of. For the most part the hillsides are covered in heath.

North portion of loop

From the east side of the Graveyard Fields' Parking Area, take the steps leading down to this paved trail. In approximately .2 of a mile cross the bridge over Yellowstone Prong. Immediately downstream is the top of Middle Falls. To visit them, hike downstream for 700'. A steep side trail leads 300' to the base of the falls.

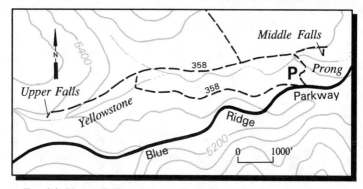

To visit Upper Falls, return to the bridge (see above) and hike the north side of the creek. This is the Graveyard Fields' Loop Trail. In .3 of a mile pass the Graveyard Ridge Trail which intersects from the right. Continue on the Graveyard Fields' Loop for another .5 of a mile, where the south portion of the loop will intersect from the left* (see below). The Upper Fall's Trail continues upstream and in approximately .2 of a mile leaves the creek's flood plain and begins its noticeable ascension of Upper Fall's Cove. Hike for another .4 of a mile, over this sometimes rubble-strewn trail to intersect the midsection of Upper Falls.

South portion of loop

The south portion of this loop trail begins at the west side of the Graveyard Fields' Parking Area.

Hike this gently descending trail and in .7 of a mile tie into the north portion of the loop, after crossing a footbridge over Yellowstone Prong* (see directions above).

Craggy Gardens Area

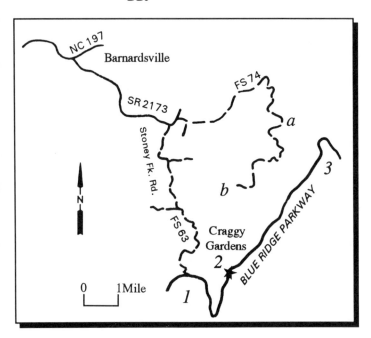

1. The Craggy Gardens Picnic Area: MP. 367.5 (approximate) Blue Ridge Parkway, access to (a) Walker and (b) Douglas Falls. Please note, this route may be gated where F.S. 63 intersects the picnic area access road. (See the text for alternate directions.)

2. The Craggy Gardens Visitor Center: MP. 364.6 Blue Ridge Parkway.

3. Glassmine Falls: MP. 361.2 Blue Ridge Parkway.

1. (a) Walker and (b) Douglas Falls, Buncombe County, N. Carolina

Roads: High Clearance   Walker Falls A "2", Douglas Falls A "4"
U.S.G.S. Quadrangles: Mt. Mitchell, Montreat, Craggy Pinnacle, N.C.
Easy, (map next pg.)

Both of these waterfalls are high on the north slope of Craggy Pinnacle and therefore don't flow heavily year-round. To see them at their best, visit after rainfall. That poses several problems though. The graveled road (F.S. 74) would be much rougher I'm sure. Its steep grades and long driving distance are trying enough when dry. The freezing and thawing of winter will heave the road making spring travel rough.

Directions: (Please note, F.S. 63 may be gated at the picnic area access road.) From the Craggy Gardens Visitor Center, MP. 364.6, drive south on the Blue Ridge Parkway for approximately 3 miles. Turn right onto the Craggy Gardens Picnic Area Access Road. In .3 of a mile turn left onto F.S. 63 (the road changes to S.R. 2178 [Stoney Fork Road] upon entering private lands). Drive down this steep and winding graveled road and in 6.8 miles arrive at Dillingham Road (S.R. 2173). Turn right and drive 1.25 miles to a one-lane bridge* (see below).

Alternate directions: From I-40 in Asheville, drive north on U.S. 19/23 to N.C. Hwy. 197 (the Barnardsville exit). Turn right onto 197 and travel 6.2 miles, passing through the community of Barnardsville, to Dillingham Road (S.R. 2173). (This intersection is approximately one-half block east of the post office.) Turn right and drive 5 miles where you'll cross a one-lane bridge* (see below).

Walker Falls
*At the above noted bridge the pavement gives way to gravel. Here you enter the Pisgah National Forest and the road is now designated F.S. 74. In .5 of a mile pass a road which intersects from the right. Drive approximately 4.3 miles to Walker Falls, which is on the left and seen from F.S. 74.

Walker Falls is a two-tier, sliding-type waterfall.

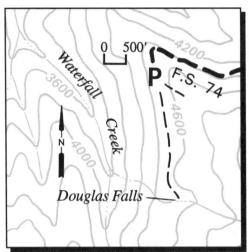

Douglas Falls

To reach Douglas Falls, continue south on F.S. 74 for an additional 4.7 miles to the parking area at the road's end. The trailhead is not marked, but as you enter the parking area it is located at the far end of the lot and to the right.

Upon entering the woods this white-blazed trail gently descends over rocky and root-laced stretches. In slightly more than .3 of a mile, pass a tremendous oak tree (portions of which are dying). It would take four people to reach around this ancient monolith. At .5 of a mile pass through an open stand of hemlock. Hike an additional .1 of a mile and arrive at an open viewing area at the base of the falls.

Douglas Falls clings to the rockface then drops a sheer 50' showering the rubble below. Hemlock flanks both sides. The rockface is 200' wide with a 20' alcove behind the falls. Beware of falling buckeyes!

2. The Craggy Gardens Visitor Center (as above).

3. Glassmine Falls,
MP. 361.2 Blue Ridge Parkway,
Buncombe County, N. Carolina

A wet-weather waterfall seen from an overlook approximately 200' from the parking area. Look due east across the valley for a half mile or so to locate the fall's cliff.

When I stopped at this location in the month of October there was no water falling over the cliff, it's too close to the ridge line for year-round flow.

Busick—Crabtree Meadows Area

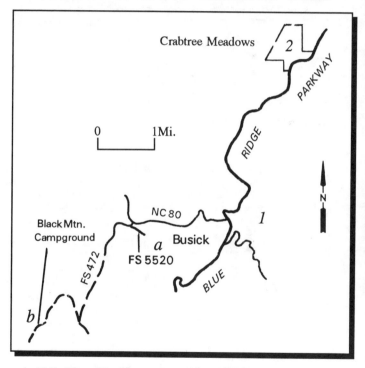

1. N.C. Hwy. 80, access to (a) Roaring Fork Falls and (b) the Falls on Setrock Creek: near MP. 344 Blue Ridge Parkway.
2. The Crabtree Meadows Campground and Visitor Center, access to Crabtree Falls: MP. 339.5 Blue Ridge Parkway.

1a. Roaring Fork Falls, Yancey County, N. Carolina

Roads: Paved   A "10"
U.S.G.S. Quadrangle: Celo, N.C.
.7 of a mile, easy

Roaring Fork is proof that a waterfall doesn't have to be big to be beautiful. More of a cascade than a waterfall, it spills five feet at a time over emerald-green, moss-covered rock ledges.

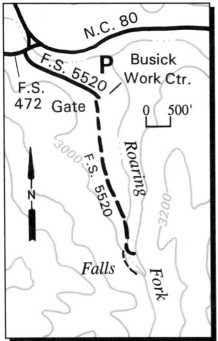

Directions: From the Blue Ridge Parkway and N.C. Hwy. 80, drive west on N.C. 80. As you pass under the parkway start your mileage check. In 2.2 miles, after passing through the community of Busick, arrive at F.S. 472*. Turn left, pass through the yield sign and cross Still Fork Creek on a small bridge. In less than .1 of a mile turn left onto F.S. 5520 (sign: "Busick Work Center"). Drive .2 of a mile and arrive at the work center. Park on the left shoulder, in the parking area provided, so as to not block the gates. Look for the gated road on the right (F.S. 5520) which serves as the fall's trail.

Hike uphill and soon pass two small concrete outbuildings. In .6 of a mile arrive at a culvert through which Roaring Fork flows. Look for the trail marker and trail on the right (west) side of the creek. Hike upstream an additional 250' to the base area.

*See the Falls on Setrock Creek.

1b. Falls on Setrock Creek, Yancey County, N. Carolina

Roads: Graveled   An "8" 60'
U.S.G.S. Quadrangle: Old Fort, N.C.
.5 of a mile, easy

Note: This beautiful wet-weather waterfall is easily reached via the Black Mountain Campground Access Road. Please park at the Black Mountain Campground Parking Area unless you are using the camping facilities.

Directions: See directions to Roaring Fork then proceed south on F.S. 472 from N.C. 80. In 1 mile the pavement ends. At 2.3 miles the road forks (in the vicinity of Neal's Creek Information Station).

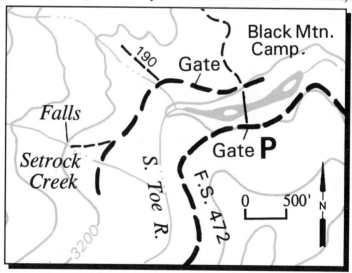

At this fork turn sharply right and continue .65 of a mile to the Black Mountain Campground Parking Area, which is on the left. The trail begins at a gated bridge on the right which crosses the South Toe River.

Cross the river and hike the graveled road on the left (west) toward the Briar Bottom Group Camp. In .2 of a mile pass another gate and soon thereafter the Mount Mitchell Trail (#190). Continue for another 800' to the Setrock Creek Fall's Trail on the right. Enter the woods and hike an additional 700' to the base of the falls.

As you get close to the falls check out the hillside covered in ferns. Another eye catcher was the overhanging trees into which the falls seem to disappear.

2. Crabtree Falls,
MP. 339.5 Blue Ridge Parkway,
Yancey County, N. Carolina

Roads: Paved   A "10" 60' Seasonal gas, food, and restrooms
U.S.G.S. Quadrangle: Celo, N.C.
.9 of a mile, moderate-difficult

Note: The trail is steep and rocky, requiring good ankle support.
Directions: From the Blue Ridge Parkway turn left (north) and

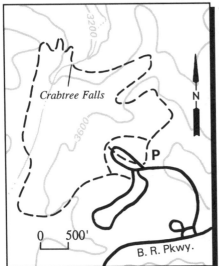

drive .35 of a mile to the campground check-in kiosk. The parking area and trailhead are on the immediate right.

Enter the woods at the northeast corner of the parking lot. In 800' a trail from the campground joins from the left. At .4 of a mile descend the first flight of stairs. At their landing the trail bends sharply left. Here, the falls can be heard in the distance. At .6 of a mile arrive at two flights of stairs. Hike another .3 of a mile to the bridge and viewing area at the base of the falls.

This captivating beauty adorns postcards found in shops up and down the parkway. Set in a heavily shaded cove, Crabtree Falls is composed of hundreds of tiny whitewater rivulets flowing down a black rock face. There is always ample water and scenery here.

Elk Park Area

Elk River Falls,
Avery County, N. Carolina

Roads: Graveled A "5" 30'
U.S.G.S. Quadrangle: Elk Park, N.C.-Tenn.
.2 of a mile, easy, (no hiking map needed)

Note: Beware of the fast and deep waters of the plunge pool.
Directions: From the intersection of U.S. Hwy. 19E and N. C. Hwy. 194 near Elk Park, N. Carolina, drive north on U.S. 19E for 1.3 miles to S.R. 1303. Turn right and drive .25 of a mile to S.R. 1305

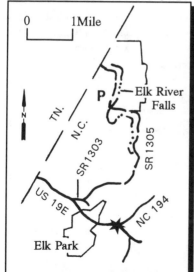

(a residential street). Turn left. After driving 2.3 miles the pavement ends. Continue for a total of 4.1 miles to the parking area. The trail begins at the north end of the parking area.

Hike .1 of a mile to a viewing area at the top of the falls. The best view, however, is at the base. To reach it, continue downstream via steps passing by a large boulder outcrop. In 300' arrive at the plunge pool.

The scenic Elk River pours over a wide and smooth rock face. The plunge pool is large, deep, and somewhat contained by bedrock and huge boulders.

Linville Falls—Wilson Creek Area

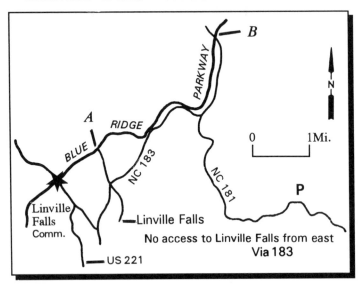

Directions: From the intersection of U.S. 221 and the Blue Ridge Parkway, north of the *community* of Linville Falls, drive north on the Blue Ridge Parkway to the following points of interest (milepost locations are approximate):

A. The Blue Ridge Parkway Spur (MP. 316.4) access to Linville Falls: 1.1 miles.

B. N.C. Hwy. 181 (MP. 312.1) access to Upper Creek Falls: 5.5 miles.

C. S.R. 1518 (MP. 311.1) access to the falls in the Kawana and Lost Cove Area (see map "C-D" pg. 77 for local detail): 6.5 miles.

D. S.R. 1511 (MP. 307.9) access to the falls in the Roseboro and Mortimer Area (see map "C-D" pg. 77 for local detail, text for this route begins on pg. 83): 9.75 miles.

A. Linville Falls,
MP. 316.4 Blue Ridge Parkway,
Burke County, N. Carolina

Roads: Paved A "10+" 15' & 45' respectively
Map: Linville Gorge Wilderness, or handout at visitor center
Easy to difficult, distances given are from the visitor center

This rugged and scenic gorge with its beautiful waterfalls is one of the Blue Ridge Parkway's main attractions, hosting thousands of visitors each year. You could spend the whole day here going from overlook to overlook. In my opinion, the finest sight here is the Lower Falls when viewed from the base. If you can handle this difficult hike, I urge you to do so. Once in a lifetime memories are waiting for you there.

The river, gorge, and falls were named for explorer William Linville, and his son John, who died at the hands of local Indians. The Linville River was called "Eeseeoh" by the Cherokee which means "a river of many cliffs."

Efforts to protect the area were made as early as the 1880's. All failed due to the lack of public funds. In 1950 John D. Rockefeller Jr. was pursuaded of the area's importance by a photograph wielding Parkway Superintendent named Sam Weems. Mr. Rockefeller donated $100,000 to purchase the falls and gorge for inclusion into the Blue Ridge Parkway. The gorge was given wilderness status in 1951, and was incorporated into the National Wilderness System in 1964. Today some 10,975 acres are protected here.

Directions: Take the Blue Ridge Parkway Spur south for 1.4 miles to the parking area and visitor center. The trails originate here.

The scenic gorge, home to Linville Falls, offers hikes for all ages and abilities. For those *not acclimated* to hiking, I suggest the .5 of a mile (easy) hike to the Upper Falls and if possible the .7 of a mile (moderate) hike to Chimney View (the first overlook from which the Lower Falls are viewed). The other overlooks and base are rated from moderate to difficult.

73

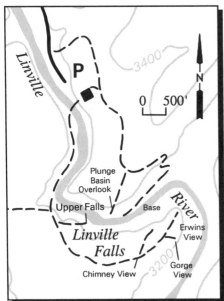

Gorge View provides you with a vista of the mountains to the south and a brief glimpse of the Linville River far below.

Erwin's View gives you a long-distance view (2000' or more) of the Lower Falls and its plunge basin, as well as the spectacular gorge. Much of the area's beauty is owed to the Erwin Quartzite walls flanking the river.

On the opposite side of the gorge is the .5 of a mile (moderate) hike to the Plunge Basin Overlook. Here you'll find a cliff-top perch offering a side view of the Lower Falls.

To reach the basin itself, return to the main trail and hike an additional .3 to .4 of a mile downstream and into the gorge.

En route you'll pass through a split boulder, then take a flight of stairs leading down. The trail is very rocky from here on and turns upstream to pass by a huge and dazzling rock wall covered in mosses and lichens. Continue over the rubble-strewn trail to the basin area and observe the beautiful Linville River falling between tarnished copper-colored cliffs. On a blue-sky day it's super!

Wilson Creek Area

The Wilson Creek Area holds some of the Blue Ridge Parkway's best kept secrets. The drive up the Wilson Creek Drainage begins alongside a wide and slow moving creek flowing through private lands, and ends with fast running tributaries high on the slopes of Grandmother and Grandfather Mountains. Aside from having many beautiful creeks and waterfalls, the hardwood-covered mountainsides are also very scenic with rocky cliffs like the Big and Little Lost Cove Cliffs, which may be seen from the Blue Ridge Parkway.

The Wilson Creek Trail System was developed to take pressure off the heavily used Shining Rock Wilderness. It seems that Wilson Creek hasn't caught on. If you're looking for a remote locale with plenty of scenery, you've just found it.

In the spring, wildflowers such as crested dwarf iris, firepink, jack-in-the-pulpit, violet, and at least three varieties of trillium are found along many of the area's streams. Trees native to the area are oak, hickory, maple, beech, american holly, hemlock, white pine, and fraser magnolia. In May, catawba rhododendron is in bloom followed by the laurels which bloom in June.

The Wilson Creek Area has many trophy trout streams and is a haven for wildlife—home to turkey, deer, and bear. The spotted sandpiper may be seen streamside, hopping from rock to rock, searching for food, comically bobbing all the while.

South of the Upper Creek Fall's Parking Area on N.C. 181 is the Brown Mountain Overlook, where it is said that the Brown Mountain Lights shimmer on nights when conditions are right. According to local folklore the lights shine from a slave's lantern as he looks for his lost master.

Near the community of Mortimer are the ruins of an old mill. The mill was destroyed by a flood in 1940. What astounds me is that the area had any commerce that long ago—it's that remote.

B. Upper Creek Falls,
Burke County, N. Carolina

Roads: Paved   A "10" 30' with shoals below
U.S.G.S. Quadrangle: Chestnut Mtn., N.C.
Trail #268B, .5 of a mile, water crossing, moderate-difficult

---

In my opinion this is the most scenic waterfall in the Wilson Creek Area.

Directions: From the Blue Ridge Parkway take N.C. Hwy. 181 south for approximately 6 miles. The Upper Creek Fall's Parking Area is on the left. The trail begins on the west side of the parking area.

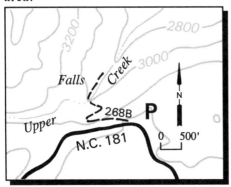

As you enter the woods, the orange-blazed trail ascends for .1 of a mile while it parallels Hwy. 181. The falls can be heard in this area. At .2 of a mile the trail switchbacks steeply downhill on its way to the top of the falls which are another .2 of a mile away.

Upon arriving creekside, look upstream for a small shoaling-type waterfall in the distance. Upper Creek then rushes through a maze of large boulders and out onto slick rock before spilling into the valley below. Atop the falls is a fine view of Cold Mountain and Simmons' Ridge to the north and Sugar Knob to the northeast.

To reach the base area, look for the trail entering the laurel on the north side of the creek. (Directly across from where you exited the woods when you arrived at the creek.) Rock-hop across the creek and hike down the steep mountainside. In 300' notice an opening where the falls are viewed from the side.

Return to the main trail and continue downhill to the base (another 300' away).

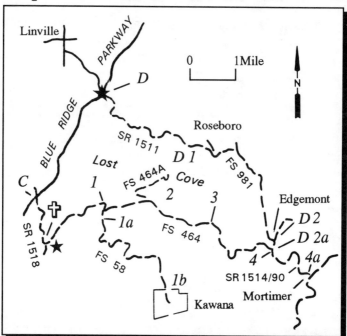

Map "C-D" Kawana and Lost Cove Area

Blue Ridge Parkway

C. Directions: From the Blue Ridge Parkway take S.R. 1518 (a graveled road) for 1.75 miles to Long Ridge Church. F.S. 464 is straight ahead. Check your mileage from the church and take F.S. 464 to access the following points of interest:

1. F.S. 58, access to (a) North Harper Creek Falls and (b) South Harper Creek Falls: 2.55 miles.
2. F.S. 464A, access to the Falls on Little Lost Cove Creek: 4.1 miles.
3. The parking area and trailhead for Hunt Fish Falls: 6.35 miles.
4. The intersection of S.R. 1514/90, south of Edgemont (also see location D2a. on the Roseboro and Mortimer Area route pg. 83): 9.5 miles. Take S.R. 1514/90 south to:
    4a. The Mortimer Work Center, access to the Falls on Thorp's Creek: 1.8 miles.

77

1. The intersection of F.S. 58 (as above).

1a. North Harper Creek Falls, Avery County, N. Carolina

Roads: Graveled   An "8" 25'
U.S.G.S. Quadrangle: Chestnut Mtn., N.C.
Trail #'s 239 & 266, 1 mile, water crossings, moderate-difficult

Directions: From the intersection of F.S. 58 and F.S. 464, drive south on F.S. 58 for .2 of a mile. Look for the parking area and trailhead on the left. Park here.

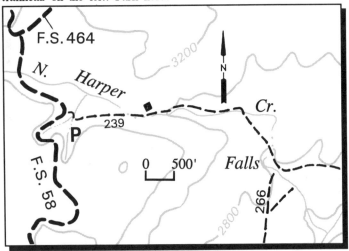

As you enter the woods, the trail descends then crosses a small unnamed branch. The trail parallels private property (denoted by the red painted trees) and in .2 of a mile crosses North Harper Creek dryshod. The next .2 of a mile is rugged walking on slick rock, rubble, roots, and through an occasional mudhole. At .6 of a mile, the trail passes through a camping area and crosses North Harper Creek on convenient stepping stones. At .7 of a mile, cross the creek again. In another .1 of a mile arrive at the top of the falls.

There is a small camping area here with a view of the North Harper Creek Valley and a distant Simmons' Ridge. The creek here is shoaling over a wide expanse of barren rock.

Most people end their trek here, missing out on the best part altogether. The base of the falls is an additional .2 of a mile further downstream and is easily accessed.

To reach the base, return to the camping area (top of the falls) and look across the creek for an opening in the laurel. Hop the creek and hike downstream for .1 of a mile to a side trail on the left. This leads to the base of the falls (another .1 of a mile away).

North Harper Creek cascades down a rock face for 200' then drops 25' into a small wooded pool.

1b. South Harper Creek Falls, Avery County, N. Carolina

Roads: Graveled/High Clearance   A "10"
U.S.G.S. Quadrangle: Chestnut Mtn., N.C.
Trail #260, 1.5 miles, moderate-difficult

Note: After driving 2.6 miles, F.S. 58 gets pretty rough, it can be driven, if careful, in an automobile with good clearance.

Directions: Drive south on F.S. 58 for a total of 4.3 miles to the parking area on the right (west) side of the road. The trailhead is on the *east side* of F.S. 58, and may be marked with a wooden sign.

Upon entering the woods, the trail descends into a hollow where it turns north while leveling out. Soon the trail turns south, completing its outline of the hollow. Now paralleling the south crest of Simmons' Ridge, in .6 of a mile intersect a path on the right that leads to private property. The South Harper Creek Trail turns sharply left here. At 1.1 miles reach another pathway which also leads to private property. Stay left here as well. Soon you'll pass red painted "bearing trees" with a beautiful view of the community of Kawana. One and four-tenths miles into the hike, pass another group of "bearing trees." The trail now starts its steep descent to

South Harper Creek. Nearing the creek, the trail switchbacks then intersects with the Raider Camp Trail. Stay left and follow the creek downstream for approximately 300', then make your way to the base area.

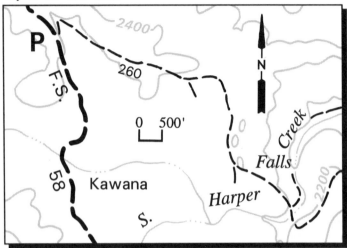

The gorge's rock walls (the highest in the Wilson Creek Area) are streaked with mineral stains. Catawba rhododendron and a few trees have managed a toehold in the fissured cliff walls. All of this adds up to a very beautiful setting, the waterfall is only a small part of it.

2. Falls on Little Lost Cove Creek, Avery County, N. Carolina

Roads: Graveled   Upper A "6"   Lower A "4"
U.S.G.S. Quadrangle: Grandfather Mtn., N.C.
No official trail, 1.5 miles, moderate-difficult

Park at the gate. Hike an undulating F.S. 464A. In .65 of a mile the road crosses Little Lost Cove Creek. At .9 of a mile pass a large opening (camping area) on the right. Continue northeast on 464A for a total of 1.4 miles. Look very carefully for a path on the right bushwacked into the laurel. This path intersects 464A at a ninety degree angle. Take the path, which leads steeply downhill, for .1 of a mile to an overgrown logging road alongside the upper falls.

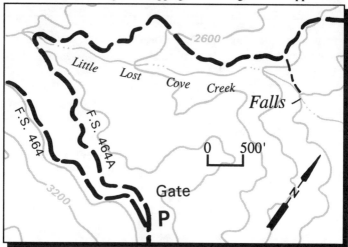

To view the upper falls from the base, you'll have to descend the bank and cross the creek (a large boulder hides their view from the path).

The upper falls are small (20'), but I think the more scenic of the two. Located in a cool, heavily shaded cove, there is an abundance of moss-covered rock. The clear, sandy-bottomed creek then disappears into the woods flowing on its way to the lower, shoaling falls.

To reach them, return to the path (overgrown logging road) and hike downstream .1 of a mile to their base.

3. Hunt Fish Falls,
Avery County, N. Carolina

Roads: Graveled A "2" 10' two tiers
U.S.G.S. Quadrangle: Chestnut Mountain, N.C.
Trail #263, .8 of a mile, minor water crossings, moderate-difficult

At this location look for the trailhead on the east side of the parking lot.

The trail winds while descending steeply. In .3 of a mile the trail

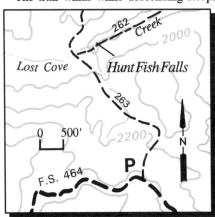

joins a small branch which it also crosses several times. At .7 of a mile intersect the Lost Cove Creek Trail (#262). Turn right and hike downstream alongside Lost Cove Creek. In 300' arrive at a large and smooth area of bedrock. The upper portion of the falls are seen on the left, while you stand atop the lower, sliding portion of the falls.

4. S.R. 1514/90 (as above). Also see D2a.
Roseboro and Mortimer Area pg. 83.

4a. Falls on Thorp's Creek,
Caldwell County, N. Carolina

Roads: Graveled A "4" 10'
U.S.G.S. Quadrangle: Chestnut Mtn., N.C.
Trail #279, .2 of a mile, easy

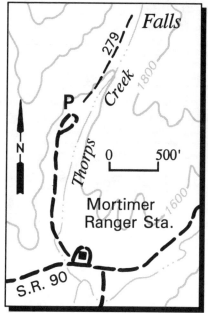

Directions: From the entrance to the Mortimer Campground and S.R. 90, drive .3 of a mile to the road's apex (loop road) and park. The trail begins here.

Follow Thorp's Creek upstream for .2 of a mile to the base of this small but very ornate waterfall.

Be very careful while trying to get a frontal view. The bedrock in front of the falls looks deceptively safe, while being treacherously slick.

Roseboro and Mortimer Area

D. Directions: From the Blue Ridge Parkway take S.R. 1511/F.S. 981 (a graveled road) to the following points of interest. (Apply the directions below to map "C-D" pg. 77.)

D1. The concrete bridge spanning Gragg Prong, access to the Falls on Gragg Prong: 4.8 miles.

D2. The intersection of S.R. 1514/90 at the community of Edgemont: approximately 9 miles. From this intersection drive south on S.R. 90 the following distance to:

    D2a. The intersection of F.S. 464: .2 of a mile. (Same as location #4, Kawana and Lost Cove Area pg. 77.)

D1. Falls on Gragg Prong,
Avery County, N. Carolina

Roads: Graveled   A "6"
U.S.G.S. Quadrangle: Grandfather Mtn., N.C.
Trail #262, 1.5 miles, water crossings, moderate

Directions: Just before crossing the concrete bridge at this location, look for a dirt road (on the west side of the bridge) that parallels Gragg Prong downstream. Drive this road 200' to its end

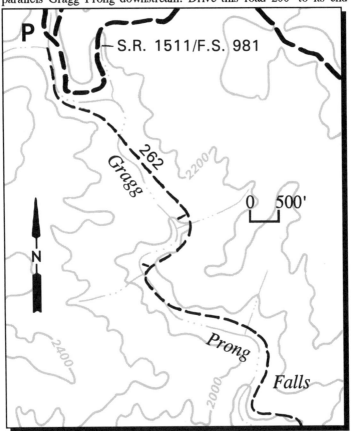

and park. The trail begins creekside at the tree line. Look for the white blazes that denote the trail.

Upon entering the woods cross a small branch. In 150' or so, reach a rocky stretch of the trail. Soon the trail turns uphill to cross a small ridge. At .2 of a mile it rejoins Gragg Prong. Four-tenths of a mile into the hike cross the creek via stepping stones and a small island. At .6 of a mile pass a small camping area on the left. Next, the trail ascends, tops out, then descends. On the downhill stretch (.7 of a mile) look carefully for a side trail on the right. This leads 200' to a beautiful rock outcrop and a 10' sliding waterfall that you'll not want to miss.

Return to the main trail and continue downstream. Soon the trail bottoms out then turns uphill after crossing two small branches. After a right turn, the trail bends left and rejoins the creek. At .9 of a mile, the trail is high above the creek. Here you'll find a 30' side trail leading to an overlook of the creek's magnificent bedrock. At 1 mile, the trail crosses Gragg Prong and immediately downstream a small tributary intersects from the right. Follow this small tributary for 30'. Here the trail re-enters the woods. After passing through a small opening, cross Gragg Prong on stepping stones to the east bank. At 1.2 miles enter a beautiful open spot with lots of rock. Notice too, the small falls here which are followed by a cascading rush through boulders. At 1.4 miles encounter a root-laced and rocky portion of the trail, followed by a small branch crossing. Continue another .1 of a mile to a side trail leading to the top of the falls.

Looking downstream you'll find an open view of the beautiful boulder-strewn gorge. The falls are typical for this region. The smooth and bare rock is evidence of high water levels.

D2. S.R. 1514/90 (as above).

D2a. F.S. 464 (as above).

Blowing Rock Area
MP. 294.7 Blue Ridge Parkway

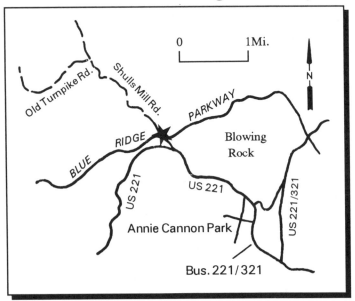

Old Turnpike Rd.

Shulls Mill Rd.

PARKWAY

BLUE RIDGE

Blowing Rock

US 221

US 221

Annie Cannon Park

US 221/321

Bus. 221/321

0   1Mi.

N

Hebron Falls, Watauga County, N. Carolina

Roads: Graveled A "5"
U.S.G.S. Quadrangle: Boone, N.C.
.5 of a mile, 20 minutes, water crossings, easy-moderate

Note: This waterfall is very different from others in the area. The cove below the falls is littered with scores of massive boulders. For a full view of them, you'll have to do some tricky boulder hopping.

Directions: From the Blue Ridge Parkway north of Blowing Rock, N. Carolina, take the U.S. 221 (Flannery Road—Shull's Mill Road) exit. At the first stop sign turn right onto Shull's Mill Road (S.R. 1552). Drive north and check your mileage when passing under the Blue Ridge Parkway overpass. In 2 miles arrive at Old Turnpike Road (S.R. 1558). Turn left and drive 1.35 miles to a pullout on the right. Park here. (If you pass the "Grace Home" you've gone too far.) The unmarked trail is directly across the road from the pullout.

From the parking area, the trail leads downhill on an old logging

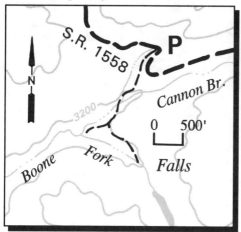

road then parallels a small unnamed branch. In .2 of a mile the trail crosses this branch. Shortly, the unnamed branch joins Cannon Branch and the trail crosses below their confluence. In another .1 of a mile the trail forks left at a large rock and now parallels Boone Fork upstream.

Traveling up Boone Fork is a little difficult, as the trail is forced onto the rubble-like boulders in the creek itself, by impassable laurel thickets and a small cliff.

A portion of the falls can be seen as you arrive at the creek bank. For a full view, however, you'll need to do some boulder hopping. Continue upstream 800' to view the falls.

Glen Burney and Glen Marie Falls, Watauga and Caldwell Counties, N. Carolina

Roads: Paved   A "5" & A "6" respectively
U.S.G.S. Quadrangles: Globe, Boone, N.C., in their margins
1.2 miles, minor water crossings, difficult

Not far from downtown Blowing Rock lie two very picturesque waterfalls. Don't let the fact that they're near town deceive you into thinking that they're somehow citified. The falls are pristine and the trail is fairly difficult.

Directions: From the intersection of U.S. 221 and Bus. 321 in Blowing Rock, drive south on Bus. 321 (Main St.) for .15 of a mile to Laurel Lane. Turn right and drive .1 of a mile. After crossing Wallingford St., look for the Annie L. Cannon Memorial Park on the left. Park here. Look for the trailhead at the south end of the parking lot.

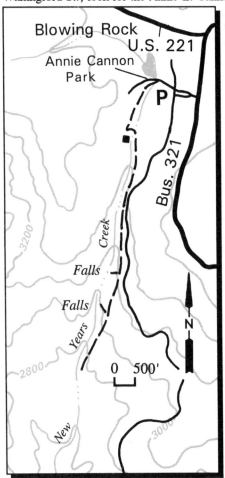

Hike 150' and cross New Year's Creek on stepping stones. The trail parallels private property and in .3 of a mile, on a series of switchbacks, descends to pass by the ruins of an old sewage treatment plant. Soon a trail intersects from the left. This leads to private property. Stay to the right. At .5 of a mile cross the creek, this time on a footbridge. In this area the trail parallels the Globe Road. At .7 of a mile reach the top of a small waterfall known as "The Cascades." A full view of them awaits you just downstream.

At .9 of a mile reach the picnic area and observation deck atop Glen Burney Falls. The only part of the falls which can be seen here is their race to the cliff edge. Just shy of a mile, pass a trail on the left that leads to private property. The main trail begins its steep descent via a series of switchbacks. At 1 mile reach the rocky side trail that leads 300' to the base of Glen Burney Falls.

Glen Burney slides and falls for 35', with a sheer drop of about 12'.

To reach Glen Marie Falls, return to the main trail and continue downstream for .2 of a mile. After descending the switchbacks take a side trail which leads to the base (slightly more than 100' away).

Glen Marie is 50' high falling in two tiers, with large boulders at the base.

MP. 272—268 Blue Ridge Parkway

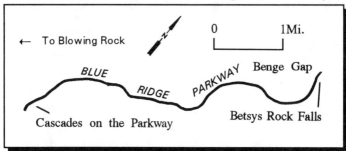

Cascades on the Parkway, Loop Trail, Wilkes County, N. Carolina

Roads: Paved A "10" 80'
U.S.G.S. Quadrangle: Maple Springs, N.C.
1 mile round trip, easy-moderate

I almost passed this waterfall up—the name "Cascades" gave me visions of a series of rapids. As is usually the case, my preconceived notions were totally wrong. The "Cascades" are *the* prize gem of the region. I commend the National Park Service for their hard work. Not only was the waterfall a magnificent sight, the trail was beautiful, spotless, and informative as well. There are plaques along the way that identify most of the trees and flowers.

Plan to spend at least two hours here. There is so much to see and learn.

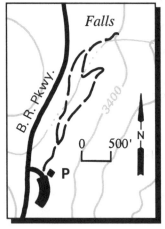

Directions: From the town of Blowing Rock, N. Carolina, drive north on the Blue Ridge Parkway to milepost 272. The parking area and trailhead are located here. The paved trail begins at the information board near the restrooms.

Begin your walk on the right fork of the trail. You will make the loop in a counterclockwise direction. After hiking .3 of a mile, reach steps leading down to Falls Creek. Just ahead, the trail crosses a footbridge and soon thereafter intersects the return portion of the loop on the left, and the fall's trail on the right. Hike the fall's trail, which now descends steps, and in .1 of a mile take a side trail to the observation area atop the falls.

Return to the steps and hike another 200' to the lower viewpoint.

This is a spectacular waterfall, falling in two tiers with shoals below.

To complete the loop, take the return trail, which soon crosses Falls Creek. In .3 of a mile rejoin the portion of the loop taken earlier. A right turn leads back to the parking area.

Betsey's Rock Falls, Wilkes County, N. Carolina

Roads: Paved   A "2"
U.S.G.S. Quadrangle: Glendale Springs, N.C.

Located near Benge Gap and MP. 268 (see map pg. 89) this high and slim waterfall is visible from a parkway overlook. Look for the sign marking their location. To view them, look southeast 1000' or so across the ravine.

Picnic facilities are also located here.

Western South Carolina

This region was a big surprise to me. I had no concept of all the scenery it held in store. This is a land of rolling hills with an occasional "knob" rising high above the surrounding terrain. This is where the foothills end and the Appalachian Mountains begin. Sunday drives abound in this land of fine homes and apple orchards.

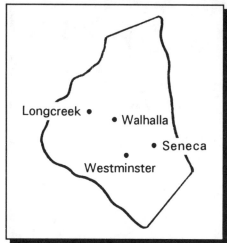

South Carolina may not have the lofty mountains of its neighboring state to the north, but it does have some equally stunning waterfalls. Most of them covered in this section of the book (unless otherwise noted) are located in Oconee County—South Carolina's "Land of Waterfalls." My favorites are the Falls on Yellow Branch and Lee Falls.

Many consider Lee Falls to be the prettiest in Oconee County. I'm partial to the Falls on Yellow Branch myself. I urge you to see them both in person and be your own judge. To see them at their best, go during the week—a time when you'll find few, if any people.

For the "history buff" there is plenty here too. Historic Oconee Station, the Stumphouse Tunnel and on the way to Lee Falls, the site on which Revolutionary War hero, General Andrew Pickens, built his home "Redhouse."

Holly Springs—Longcreek Area

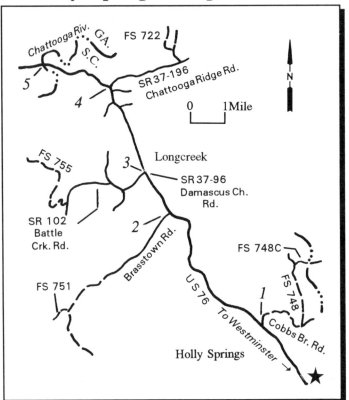

Directions: From the intersection of U.S. Hwys. 76 *West* and 123 *South* in Westminster, S.C., drive west on 76 to the following points of interest:

1. Cobb's Bridge Road, access to Rileymoore Falls: 7.35 miles.
2. Brasstown Road (S.R. 48), access to Brasstown Falls: 11.9 miles.
3. Damascus Church Road (S.R. 37-96), access to Long Creek Falls: 13.2 miles.

4. Chattooga Ridge Road (S.R. 37-196), access to Fall Creek Falls: 15.7 miles.

5. The Chattooga River Bridge (Ga./S.C. state line): 17.9 miles.

1. Rileymoore Falls

Roads: Graveled/4 WD   A "3" 8'
U.S.G.S. Quadrangle: Holly Springs, S.C.
1.15 miles, moderate-difficult

Directions: From U.S. 76 drive east on Cobb's Bridge Road for 1.4 miles. Turn left onto Spy Rock Road (F.S. 748) and drive 1.85 miles to F.S. 748C. Turn right onto 748C and continue for .1 of a mile to the parking area on the right. The road is steep and deeply rutted from this point and requires a 4 WD vehicle to reach the new trailhead.

From the parking area, hike east on 748C. The road bends south as it descends into the Chauga River Valley. In .45 of a mile the road forks. Take the right fork for 250', passing the high-clearance parking area, en route to the new hiking trail on the left. Enter the woods and hike the winding trail an additional .65 of a mile to the falls.

2. Brasstown Falls

Roads: Graveled   An "8" collectively
U.S.G.S. Quadrangle: Tugaloo Lake, Ga.- S.C.
.2 of a mile, easy-moderate

Directions: From U.S. 76, turn left (south) onto Brasstown

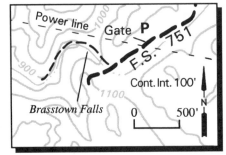

Road (S.R. 48). Drive 4.1 miles to F.S. 751. Turn right and drive .5 of a mile to the parking area and trailhead. The trail begins at the gate (guardrail).

Hike the gated road and immediately pass under a power line. In 200' the road enters the woods.

In another 300' veer right at a camping area. Hike an additional 200' to a shoaling Brasstown Creek. The first of three falls are immediately downstream.

There is a right and wrong way to the base of each of these falls. The wrong way is to try to take *any* route from the top area of either of the three falls. These trails are steep, slick, and dangerous.

The correct route is a slim trail *farthest* from the creek. This trail provides access to the base of both the upper and middle falls, then eventually leads steeply to the base of the lower falls.

The upper falls are the more scenic of the three. Brasstown Creek spills from ledge to ledge for a total of 40' over a broad rock face and then shoals 125' racing to make its next plunge.

The middle falls resemble a wide and uniform curtain of water with a powerful sheer drop of 15'. The morning sun's rays show through its mist laden air. Approaching the base is a drenching experience.

The lower falls tumble for 15' into a bowl-shaped alcove. This is another of those locations where the waterfall is only a small portion of the big picture. There is a 70' multi-colored rock wall across the plunge pool playing host to dozens of aquatic plants. Altogether, it's a tremendous sight.

Upper Brasstown Falls

Long Creek Falls

3. Long Creek Falls

Roads: Graveled/High Clearance   A "6" 30'
U.S.G.S. Quadrangle: Rainy Mountain, Ga.-S.C.
1.5 miles, moderate

Directions: From U.S. Hwy. 76, turn left (south) onto Damascus Church Road (S.R. 37-96, the Longcreek Volunteer Fire Dept. is located at this intersection) and drive for .85 of a mile. Turn right onto Battle Creek Road (S.R. 37-102) and drive 1.9 miles to Turkey Ridge Road (F.S. 755). Turn right (west) and continue for another 2.95 miles to the graveled parking area on the left. (If you have a high clearance vehicle and conditions are dry, F.S. 755-1, on the right, may be driven to a pullout .4 of a mile ahead.)

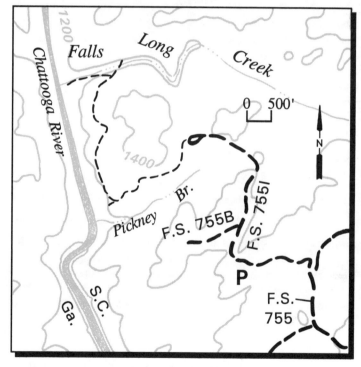

From the *graveled parking area* hike 755-1 and in .15 of a mile pass 755B on the left. In another .25 of a mile pass the high clearance pullout (mentioned above) on the right. In approximately 800' reach a point where the road that serves as the trail encounters a small knob and makes a ninety degree bend left (northwest). Hike 300' and arrive at a turnaround and camping area. Look northwesterly for the fall's trail which leads through brush and treads through a gulley before intersecting a more open logging road. Here, the trail rounds the north side of a small knob before paralleling Pickney Branch. In .6 of a mile a path continues straight ahead, while the fall's trail turns right (north) to follow the distant Chattooga River upstream. One and three-tenths miles into the hike pass through the inland most point of a hollow. Continue an additional .2 of a mile to a point where the trail makes a sharp bend to the right (the rushing waters of Long Creek are heard here). Look for a side trail on the left, which leads 400' steeply down to the river's edge. Long Creek joins the Chattooga just upstream. The falls are inland approximately 300'.

4. Fall Creek Falls

Roads: Graveled   A "5" 40'
U.S.G.S. Quadrangle: Whetstone, S.C.-Ga.
5 minutes, steep-moderate

Directions: From U.S. 76 take Chattooga Ridge Road (S.R. 37-196) east for 2.1 miles to Fall Creek Road (F.S. 722). Turn left, and stay left for .85 of a mile arriving at a culvert through which Fall Creek flows. Park in a pullout just ahead on the left.

Walk the road north for 50' and look for a gulley on the left. This leads to the base of the falls and is the best way down. There is no defined trail.

5. The Chattooga River Bridge (Ga./S.C. line) as above.

Walhalla West

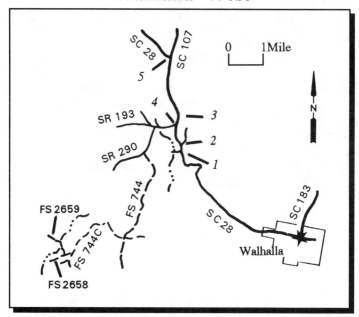

Directions: From the intersection of S.C. Hwys. 28 (Main St.) and 183 *North* in Walhalla, drive north on Hwy. 28 to the following points of interest:

1. The Yellow Branch Picnic Area, access to the Falls on Yellow Branch: 5.5 miles.
2. Stumphouse Tunnel Road (S.R. 37-226), access to Issaqueena Falls: 5.6 miles.
3. The Stumphouse Ranger Station: 6.0 miles.
4. Whetstone Road (S.R. 193), access to the Falls on Cedar Creek—Blue Hole Falls: 6.3 miles.
5. The intersection of S.C. Hwys. 28 and 107: 8.3 miles. (Also see Nicholson and Burrell's Ford Areas pg. 109.)

1. Falls on Yellow Branch

Roads: Paved   A "10 + " 60'
U.S.G.S. Quadrangle: Whetstone, S.C.-Ga.
No formal trail, 1 mile to base, shallow water crossings, moderate

Note: This grand spectacle takes extra ability in the trail finding department. The trail is easy to discern in places, then in others seems to vanish. Hang tough, the rewards are great!

Directions: From Hwy. 28 turn left into the Yellow Branch Picnic Area. Drive less than .1 of a mile to the pullout on the left. Park here. (If you cross Yellow Branch and enter the parking lot for the #2 picnic area, you've gone too far.) The trail may be marked by a sign, 100' or so due south, reading "nature trail." If the sign is missing,

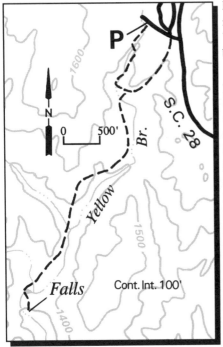

look for a small collapsed rock bridge and cross Yellow Branch over it to begin your hike.

Hike downstream, paralleling Yellow Branch and crossing the creek *four* times. Slightly more than .2 of a mile into the hike, where the loop trail veers left (east), away from Yellow Branch, look carefully for a faint trail on the right (south side). This trail leads to the falls. (The loop trail continues ahead for .2 of a mile and returns to the #1 picnic area.)

Hike the side trail and in 125' cross Yellow Branch.

In .2 of a mile, reach a portion of the trail that treads upon an old logging road for a short distance. At a point .6 of a mile into the hike, there are trees that have fallen in line with the trail, obscuring it. At .8 of a mile the trail leaves Yellow Branch and climbs a small ridge. After topping out, the trail descends its west slope and then crosses a small branch at its confluence with Yellow Branch. A small pool is located here. Approximately 200' downstream from the pool, cross Yellow Branch on shallow bedrock. (The trail is hard to discern here because people have taken different routes across the creek.) Now on the east side of the creek, continue 200' downstream to the top of the falls. The top has several hazards: first, it's 60' straight down; and second, a bumper crop of industrial-strength poison ivy. Hazards aside, there is a fine view of the forest below.

To reach the base, take the steep and muddy trail on the left downstream another 250'.

2. Issaqueena Falls

Roads: Paved   A "10" 50'
U.S.G.S. Quadrangle: Walhalla, S.C.
.1 of a mile, 10 minutes, moderate
Open 8:00 a.m. to dusk, poison ivy, (no hiking map needed)

This awesome beauty is located within South Carolina's historic Stumphouse Tunnel Park. Stumphouse Mountain is the site of a failed 1850's railroad tunneling venture. The Blue Ridge Railroad Company had plans to connect Charleston, S.C., with Cincinnati, Ohio. A series of three tunnels were begun, but only "middle tunnel," the shortest (385') was completed. The project was put on hold in 1859 when funds dried up. The Civil War dealt it a final death blow, and work was never resumed.

Of the three tunnels, only Stumphouse Tunnel is intact. Stumphouse Tunnel was to be 5863' long. Only 1600' of it was completed. The work was performed by Irishmen, progressing 200' a month, using hand tools and black powder.

I urge you to see the tunnel after visiting picturesque Issaqueena Falls. There is even a small wet-weather cascade to the left of the tunnel opening (Tunnel Falls).

There is a story behind Issaqueena Falls as well. It is said that an Indian maiden who married a white trader jumped from the falls to her death to escape persecution from her tribe. Another version of the story says that she jumped from the top of the falls to a ledge below and then under the cover of darkness fled to Alabama to join her husband. No matter what the story, the falls are a legendary beauty when seen from the base.

Directions: Turn right onto a winding and steeply-descending Stumphouse Tunnel Road (S.R. 37-226). Drive .4 of a mile and turn right into the fall's picnic area, park at the apex of this loop road.

Hike south 200' to the top of the falls. There's not much to view from this vantage point—just another creek flowing over a cliff. The mood is altered altogether en route to the base. The setting changes to one of being deep in the woods.

To reach the base, take the trail crossing the footbridge on the *west* side of the parking lot and in approximately 400' arrive at a side trail on the left. Take this trail 200' to the base of the falls.

Hundreds of small trickles race down the granite face forming a natural masterpiece.

Stumphouse Tunnel
To visit the tunnel, return to Stumphouse Tunnel Road and drive north .2 of a mile to the gate. Park, then hike 300' to its opening.

3. The Stumphouse Ranger Station (as above).

4. Falls on Cedar Creek—Blue Hole Falls

Roads: High Clearance   A "4" & A "4"
U.S.G.S. Quadrangle: Whetstone, S.C.-Ga.
300 -400', water crossing, easy-moderate

Note: I visited these waterfalls during a summer dry spell. The water crossing at the shoals was ankle-deep. I feel certain that a little rain would make the creek faster and much deeper. I urge extreme caution here at all times, but especially under adverse conditions.

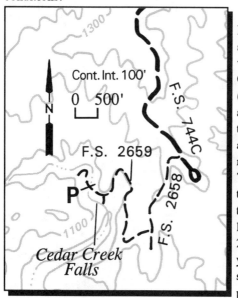

Directions: From Hwy. 28 take Whetstone Road (S.R. 193) west for .7 of a mile to Cassidy Bridge Road (S.R. 290). Turn left and drive .9 of a mile to F.S. 744. Turn left again and drive 3.3 miles to F.S. 744C. Turn right and continue for 2.55 miles to the single-lane and lightly-graveled F.S. 2658 on the right. (If you end up at a cul-de-sac on 744C you've passed 2658 by .15 of a mile.) Travel from here on should be made in a high clearance vehicle or on foot.

Turn right onto 2658 and drive .35 of a mile to F.S. 2659. Turn right again and in .2 of a mile arrive at the pullout on the left. The trail to the falls begins here.

Hike down this steep trail and exit the woods on bedrock at creek level. The Falls on Cedar Creek are directly upstream 150' or so.

This waterfall is broader than it is high, and despite heavy visitation still has an unspoiled appearance. The creek slides down the rock face, pools, then shoals its way downstream to Blue Hole Falls, which from this vantage point is hidden from view. Notice the potholes in the rock where Cedar Creek drops out of sight. Blue Hole lies just beyond them.

To reach Blue Hole Falls, return to the spot where you first arrived at the creek. Look for the shallowest route across the creek. (You can see the worn track most people have taken to cross it.) Once on the west bank, carefully walk the dry portion of the bedrock downstream. In approximately 60' the trail re-enters the woods and leads steeply downhill to a viewpoint alongside Blue Hole Falls.

Despite being easy to reach, this waterfall has a rugged beauty about it. The mountainsides are steep, craggy, and cloaked in laurel and rhododendron.

5. S.C. Hwys. 28 and 107 (as above).

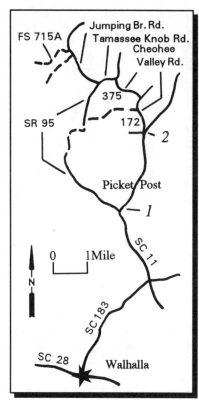

Walhalla North

Directions: From the intersection of S.C. Hwy. 28 and S.C. Hwy. 183 *North* in Walhalla, S.C., drive north on Hwy. 183 for 3.55 miles to S.C. Hwy. 11. Take Hwy. 11 north to the following points of interest:

1. Oconee Station Road (S.R. 95, sign: "Oconee Station State Historic Site"), access to Station Cove Falls: 2.1 miles.

2. Cheohee Valley Road (S.R. 172), access to Lee Falls: 4.5 miles. See the text for further directions.

1. Station Cove Falls

Roads: Paved   A "7" 60'
U.S.G.S. Quadrangle: Walhalla, S.C.
.7 of a mile, minor water crossing, easy

Directions: Turn left onto Oconee Station Road (S.R. 95) and check your mileage. In 2 miles, pass historic Oconee Station* which is on the right. Continue for another .3 of a mile (2.3 miles total) to a small off-the-road parking area on the left. The fall's trail begins here.

This well maintained trail (old logging road) enters the woods and descends while bending in an "S" fashion. In approximately .1 of a mile arrive at a sharp left turn where the trail descends to cross a footbridge. (The horse trail continues straight ahead.)

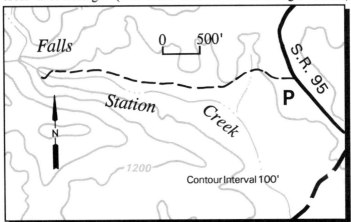

Approximately .2 of a mile into the hike pass alongside a swamp created by industrious beavers. Cross the second footbridge at .4 of a mile and in another .2 of a mile arrive at Station Creek. Cross the creek here on stepping stones. (The trail on the right dead-ends and leaves you having to cross the creek on slick rock.) Hike an additional .1 of a mile to the base of the falls.

This low country waterfall is quite different from its highland neighbors. The rock face lacks the mosses, while the forest is primarily deciduous with sparse conifers.

Oconee Station State Historic Site

While in the area, visit historic Oconee Station. (*See directions above.)

Oconee Station was one of seven outposts authorized by the South Carolina General Assembly in the 1750's to protect western frontier settlements from Indian attacks. The outpost was home to thirty militia-men at a time and soon became a thriving center of trade.

Two of the original buildings, one of which was owned by a prosperous trader (and are the oldest in Oconee County dating to around 1800), are still intact.

2. Lee Falls

Roads: Graveled   A "10" 40' (map next page)
U.S.G.S. Quadrangle: Tamassee, S.C.
1.6 miles, 1 hour, water crossings, difficult

Note: I hiked to this waterfall in the summertime. Had the wildlife openings not recently been mowed, I would've been walking through almost hip-deep grasses and vines. I would therefore recommend that you hike to Lee Falls on a mild winter's day or before new growth occurs in the spring.

Directions: Turn left (west) onto Cheohee Valley Road (S.R. 172, this changes to S.R. 375 in just over a mile) and drive 2.2 miles to Tamassee Knob Road (S.R. 95). Turn left and continue for .5 of a mile to Jumping Branch Road (County Hwy. 9). Turn right and drive 1.45 miles to F.S. 715A on the left. Travel 715A (a one-lane graveled road) for .7 of a mile to the parking area on the north side of the low bridge over Tamassee Creek. The trail treads a roadbed that follows Tamassee Creek upstream. The hike begins at the gate just upstream from the parking area.

Hike the grassy road bed (the middle route provides the best walking) through the first wildlife opening. In .2 of a mile the road (trail) veers left and crosses Tamassee Creek to the south bank. Three-tenths of a mile into the hike, you'll arrive at another wildlife opening with a test planting of hardwoods. At .4 of a mile arrive at a third wildlife opening. This opening was planted with corn when I visited. (Hike the tree line on the high side of this field for easier going.) In .2 of a mile the road exits this field and crosses to the north side of Tamassee Creek.

Enter another cultivated wildlife opening (the fourth), and walk the high side of this field as well. Seven-tenths of a mile into the hike the road re-enters the woods. At the 1 mile point the road (trail) turns uphill and narrows to a single track. In approximately 300' look carefully to the left for the narrow fall's trail (easily missed). The main trail continues up the mountainside.

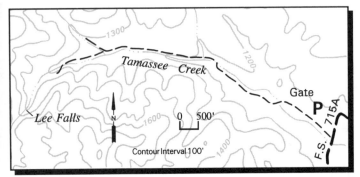

Take the fall's trail, and in approximately 200' cross a small unnamed creek. (The trail is hard to discern on the other side.) Two-tenths of a mile from the main trail, you'll arrive at a fire ring at the pointed base of a ridge. A trail here leads up the ridge— disregard it. At the fire ring cross to Tamassee Creek's south bank. Hike the creek upstream approximately 300' to the ruins of a stone gold smelter. From here on it's hunt and peck hiking in the creek. Continue for .2 of a mile to the base of the falls.

The fall's cove is steep and very beautiful, with mosses of every hue of green imaginable adorning the cliff face.

Local History

During the Revolutionary War, the Cherokee raided white settlements in the area while local Patriots were in the coastal Carolinas fighting the British. General Andrew Pickens and his forces came to the area to quash the raids. General Pickens so liked the area that he made it his home. His residence "Redhouse" sat atop a hill located at the intersection of Tamassee Knob Road and Jumping Branch Road. A boulder and plaque, placed by The Daughters of the American Revolution marks the spot.

Nicholson and Burrell's Ford Areas

Note: I have hiked the Chattooga River Trail (CRT) from Burrell's Ford downstream to the Nicholson Ford access. I measured a total distance of 8.7 miles. The CRT is rugged, especially between Big Bend Falls and the Falls on the Chattooga above Rock Gorge. I therefore recommend that you go in from either end and return to that respective trailhead instead of trying to connect all the way through.

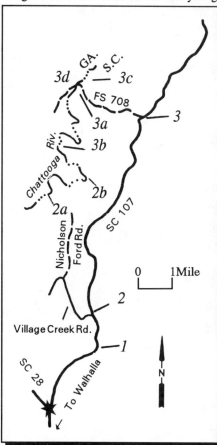

Directions: From the intersection of S.C. Hwys. 28 and 107 northwest of Walhalla, drive north on 107 the following distances to these points of interest:

1. Oconee State Park: 2.5 miles.

2. Village Creek Road, access to (a) Lick Log Creek Falls and (b) the Falls on the Chattooga River above Rock Gorge: 3.5 miles.

3. Burrell's Ford Road (F.S. 708), access to (a) King Creek, (b) Big Bend, (c) Spoonauger Falls, and (d) the Chattooga River Bridge: 10.4 miles.

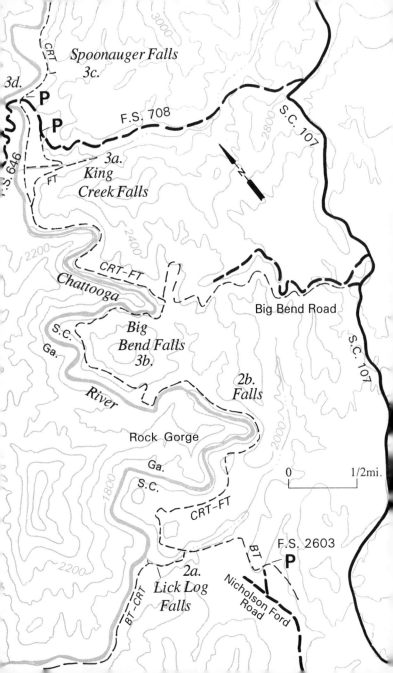

1. Oconee State Park (as above).

2a. Lick Log Creek Falls

Roads: Graveled   A "6" & "4" respectively
U.S.G.S. Quadrangle: Satolah, Tamassee, S.C.-Ga. in their margins
Yellow and white blazed, 1 mile to lower falls, moderate

Directions: From Hwy. 107, turn left (west) onto Village Creek Road and drive 1.75 miles to Nicholson Ford Road. Turn right and drive 2.1 miles, fording two small creeks while en route to F.S. 2603. Veer right onto 2603, the parking area is .15 of a mile ahead. The trail begins at the northwest corner of the lot.

Upper Falls
Enter the woods on the trail to the left (this is the Bartram Trail). This trail descends and will soon follow Lick Log Creek downstream. Soon after crossing the second footbridge pass by the audible falls. Seven-tenths of a mile into the hike intersect the CRT*. At this intersection, go left (south), then follow Lick Log Creek upstream to see the upper falls.

Lower Falls
Directly downstream from the upper falls, cross a footbridge and hike .2 of a mile passing a small waterfall which can be seen through the laurel. Approximately 150' further downstream, the CRT bends sharply left as it nears the river. Here you'll find an unmarked pathway on the right leading to the lower falls. This path is steep. The lower falls are 30' inland from the river.

*See Falls on the Chattooga River above Rock Gorge.

2b. Falls on the Chattooga River above Rock Gorge

Roads/Quadrangle: See Lick Log Creek   A "6" 15'
3.1 miles from the Lick Log parking area, moderate-difficult

At the intersection of the Bartram Trail and Chattooga River Trail*, hike north (following the CRT upstream) for 2.4 miles. From this intersection the trail gains approximately 300' in elevation as it goes up and over a ridge to the inland side of a mountain. (This mountain blocks sight and sound of the river.) In this area you'll bypass the Chattooga's Square Bends and Rock Gorge. Next, the trail traverses a ridge line while paralleling the wild and scenic river boundary (denoted by blue painted trees) for approximately a mile. At 1.75 miles the CRT turns sharply right and descends into a hollow, the sounds of the river return. While on this leg you may catch a glimpse of the river to the north. (Where the river bends left and then disappears is our objective.) The CRT turns sharply left and completes its outline of the hollow, then descends close to river level. As you approach the river, look for and make your way to a beach-like area with outcrops of bedrock. The lower left portion of the falls can be seen here. For a better view, hike upstream approximately 300' and scramble down to the river's edge where they are seen from the side.

*See Upper Lick Log Creek Falls for directions to this point.

3a. King Creek Falls

Roads: Graveled   A "7" 80'
U.S.G.S. Quadrangle: Tamassee, S.C.-Ga.
.8 of a mile, 20 minutes, easy-moderate, (map pg. 110)

Directions: From Hwy. 107, drive west on Burrell's Ford Road (F.S. 708) for 2.4 miles to the Burrell's Ford Campground Parking Area, which is on the left. Locate the information board at the northeast corner of the parking area. The trail begins here and carries its own blue blaze as well as the white blaze of the Foothills Trail.

Hike this curvaceous trail and in .5 of a mile the orange-blazed trail from the Burrell's Ford Campground joins from the right. After crossing a footbridge over King Creek the Foothills Trail departs to the right, while the now orange- and blue-blazed trail to King Creek Falls continues to the left (upstream). Hike an additional .3 of a mile to the base of the falls.

3b. Big Bend Falls

Roads: Graveled   An "8"   (map pg. 110)
U.S.G.S. Quadrangle: Tamassee, S.C.-Ga.
3.5 miles, 1 hour and 15 minutes, moderate-difficult

Directions*: From the Burrell's Ford Campground Parking Area continue west on 708 for .25 of a mile to the parking area for the Chattooga River Trail (CRT).

Hike the CRT *downstream*. In .5 of a mile cross the footbridge over King Creek. At the 1 mile point pass the fisherman's register. Here, the Foothills Trail joins from the east after a close encounter with King Creek Falls. In this area the galax-lined CRT shortcuts a bend in the river, first climbing moderately, then descending back to river level. In another .3 of a mile cross a footbridge then ascend to a point where you have an equally beautiful view, both up and down river.

One and seven-tenths miles into the hike reach the first switchbacks. Here, the trail again descends to river level. After the river bends left, you will enter a long straightaway. In this area (1.9 miles into the hike) look for a small shoal. The exposed rock here is a great place for sunning. At 2.25 miles the steep hillsides force the trail out onto the bedrock of the riverbed itself. (This portion of the trail, 300' or so, may be in shallow water after heavy rains. I've hiked this trail in both summer and winter and had no problem, but the treadway was significantly narrowed by the higher water levels of winter.) At 2.6 miles, cross a creek with a trail up its cove. This trail leads to Big Bend Road and S.C. Hwy. 107 (signs here give directions and distances). Just ahead you'll encounter the second set of switchbacks—this time ascending. Continue from the last mentioned trail intersection for .8 of a mile. As you exit a *descending* switchback, look for a slim side trail near the river's bank leading down to the fall's viewpoint.

*See King Creek Falls.

3c. Spoonauger Falls

Roads: Graveled   A "3"   (map pg. 110)
U.S.G.S. Quadrangle: Tamassee, S.C.-Ga.
.4 of a mile, 15 minutes, easy-moderate

Note: Best seen after rainfall.

Directions*: Hike the Chattooga River Trail *upstream* and in .2 of a mile cross Spoonauger Creek. Hike the fall's trail up Spoonauger Creek and in .15 of a mile arrive at the base of the falls.

*See Big Bend Falls.

3d. The Chattooga River Bridge (as above).

Caesar's Head Area

Raven Cliff Falls,
Greenville County, S. Carolina

Roads: Paved   A "10"
U.S.G.S. Quadrangle: Table Rock, S.C.
Red blaze, 2.2 miles, moderate-difficult

This waterfall is located in the Mountain Bridge Recreation and Wilderness Area near Caesar's Head State Park. Here, the Appalachian Mountains rise abruptly out of South Carolina's foothills. Witness this dramatic change in the landscape from trailside overlooks, but especially when looking to the east from the Raven Cliff's observation deck.

Directions: From the intersection of U.S. Hwys. 64 and 276 *South* in downtown Brevard, North Carolina, drive south for 14.4 miles to the parking area on the east side of U.S. 276. The trail treads the gated service road on the *west* side of 276.

Alternate Directions: If visiting Caesar's Head State Park, S.C., drive north for 1.1 miles from the visitor center to the Raven Cliff's Parking Area on the right.

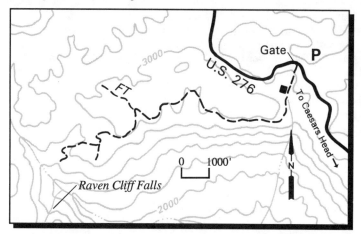

Enter the woods on the gated service road. This road carries the blue blaze of the Foothills Trail and the red blaze of the Raven Cliff Fall's Trail.

The road descends moderately and in .2 of a mile arrives at a small building. The road changes into a trail after crossing a culvert, then ascends, rounds the mountain, and levels out. Now following the mountainside much like a contour line, in .7 of a mile the trail narrows as it treads a rocky stretch, then begins a gradual ascent. (In this vicinity, the trail, which has been treading upon an old logging road, leaves that road to shortcut a hollow.) At .8 of a mile the trail makes a ninety degree bend to the right. Soon the trail bends left where it descends stairs. It then turns right at their base and descends still further. Now tracing the hollow, the trail turns steeply uphill over a root-laced stretch. At 1.1 miles the trail rejoins the logging road and levels out. In approximately .1 of a mile the trail makes a hard right atop a ridge.

One and four-tenths miles into the hike, the blue-blazed Foothills Trail turns off to the right, while the red-blazed Raven Cliff Fall's Trail leads left. Signs here denote this intersection. At 1.6 miles arrive at an open spot where the South Carolina foothills can be seen. (Raven Cliff can be seen here, but not the falls.) Notice how the foothills end and the Appalachians begin. At 1.75 miles, after having descended in an "S" fashion over a rocky stretch of trail, pass the Dismal Trail which intersects on the left. (This leads .15 of a mile to a lower, somewhat obscured view of the falls.) The fall's trail descends further and at 1.9 miles enters a canopy of rhododendron. The trail here is on the north side of the mountaintop and rounds the west side en route to the south slope. At 2 miles the trail descends steeply via a rocky switchback. In another .1 of a mile the trail makes a ninety degree left turn and continues its descent. After hiking a total of 2.2 miles arrive at the fall's observation deck.

The fall's are seen approximately 800' across the gorge. The falls leap 30' then run 200' as cascades before plunging a wind-swept 70' from Raven Cliff (a total height of 420'). I visited the falls during the dry season and there was ample water.